Plantalicious

Vegan Recipes

TRACY SADLER & SYLVIA KENIMER

Copyright © 2018 Tracy Sadler & Sylvia Kenimer
All rights reserved.
literarykeystone@gmail.com
FAO Plantalicious PR

First edition published in Great Britain by Ink Hills Ltd in 2018.
This edition published by Keystone Literary in 2019.

No part of this publication may be reproduced, distributed, or transmitted in any form or by any means, including photocopying, recording, or other electronic or mechanical methods, without the prior written permission of the publisher, except in the case of brief quotations embodied in critical reviews and certain other noncommercial uses permitted by copyright law. For permission requests contact the publisher: literarykeystone@gmail.com with "permission request" in the subject field.

This book is sold subject to the condition that it shall not, by way of trade or otherwise, be lent, resold, hired out, or otherwise circulated without the publisher's prior consent in any form of binding or cover other than that in which it is published and without a similar condition, including this condition, being imposed on the subsequent purchaser.

ISBN-13: 978-1726071161
ISBN-10: 1726071162

CONTENTS

Author Bios

The Recipes

Tracy Sadler is a Raw Vegan Alchemist and Creative Vinyasa Flow Yoga teacher. Travelling the world working on retreats, teacher trainings and workshops. Tracy's recipes are inspired by her love of travel and the different cultural dishes and foods experienced on her world adventures.

Sylvia Kenimer is a Worcestershire based American writer who has a passion for vegan cooking and believes that food is medicine. She has assisted many individuals through rehabilitation from obesity and into a sustainable and healthy lifestyle. Kenimer began her epicurean journey at home in Colorado, USA before emigrating to Spain and Italy, developing her knowledge of world food.

RECIPES

Plantacious Pizza Bases

The pizza is one of my best selling snacks at vegan fairs and festivals. I even make it for take away and deliveries in and around the midlands. The thought of being able to have pizza on a Friday night and not feel guilty, has got to be like the best thing ever. It is super nourishing and filling and you may even discover your 'non vegan' friends are after a slice or two!! Both the psyllium and flax are high in fibre helping to alleviate digestive complaints. The flax is also high in Omega-3, which is beneficial for good heart health.

Ingredients
1 Small Organic Cauliflower
250g Golden Flaxseed
1 tbs. Garlic Granules
1tsp. Rock Salt
2 tbsp. **Psyllium** Husk
750ml Filtered Water

Method
Chop cauliflower by hand or in a food processor into small rice size pieces. In a high power blender or coffee grinder blitz the flaxseed into a meal consistency. You are always better to buy the flax as a whole seed and process yourself when you need it, more likely than not pre grinded flax with be rancid. Add both cauliflower and flax to a bowl and mix in salt and garlic first before gradually adding the water and mixing continuously. The mixture should not be sloppy and not to thick either, so you may need a little more or less water. Finally add the psyllium husk and mix quickly and evenly, you will notice this starts to thicken the pizza base mixture and will give it a dough like consistency once 'baked'. Your base is now ready to spread on your Teflex dehydrator sheet. Dehydrate for 9-10 hours before flipping off the sheet and dehydrating for another 5-6 hours. You want the base still to be a little softer not too firm like a cracker.

TRACY SADLER & SYLVIA KENIMER

PLANTALICIOUS: VEGAN RECIPES

Top with your favourite seed or nut cheeze, pesto, marinated veggies or olives.

Sunflower Maca Mayo

One of my favourite places in the world is beautiful Bali. I've been blessed to spend a good few months over the past two years on the Island of The Gods. Full of magical and mystical charm, heart warming smiles from the local people and luscious vegetation and rice paddy fields. My friend Katie Holland, sacred dance extraordinaire and I hosted an amazing retreat in Bali for the first time in 2016 including snorkelling, dancing, yoga, raw food (of course) plus lots of other fantastic cultural experiences. After the retreat we were getting together one night for dinner, as usual Tracy got over excited and prepared a substantial feast of local organic salad, red rice, raw pizza, avocado and sweet potato wedges made with coconut oil. Knowing that Katie loves her condiments as much as me, I wanted to whizz together something for dunking the wedges in and so was born this recipe. To me food is all about being creative, having fun and putting my energy and enjoyment into it to then share with others. Remember you can always experiment with other seeds and nuts, try your own favourite combinations.

The benefits of Maca are monumental, providing many essential vitamins including iron, zinc and magnesium. It balances hormones, particularly for woman at menopause and can increase fertility in those trying to conceive. This Peruvian root vegetable is extremely energising, mood balancing and a good powder to add to your morning smoothies or mylks. I love its caramel almost toffee like flavour, making it very comforting and nourishing to devour!!

Ingredients
100g Sunflower Seeds- organic where possible
2 tbsp. Nutritional Yeast
2 tsp. Apple Cider Vinegar
½ tsp. Rock Salt
1 tsp. Smoked Paprika
2 tbsp. Olive Oil
1 tbsp. Coconut Oil
60ml. Filtered Water
2 tsp. Maca Powder
Method
Soak sunflower seeds in filtered water for a minimum of 4 hours, maximum of 8 hours. The soaking process helps to break down enzyme inhibitors, which act like a 'coat' on the nut or seed making it difficult for us to absorb its full range of vitamins and minerals. Soaking also makes it is easier for us to digest the nuts and seeds, giving our digestive systems a bit of a break from the already taxing and 'stressful' lifestyles we can lead.
Drain and rinse sunflower seeds well before adding to your blender along with all other ingredients apart from the coconut oil and Maca. Finally add the melted coconut oil and Maca powder. Over processing Maca can make it taste bitter, hence why we add it last. Enjoy your Maca mayo with your favourite crudities, raw crackers or breads, use as a topping for the pizza base or as Katie and I did dunk your sweet potato wedges in it!!

Nutty or Seedy Cheezes

A raw foodie stable has got to be the nut or seed cheeze, more commonly you will see raw cheeze made with cashew due to its creamy texture and high carbohydrate composition. Although I love to make and enjoy this variation from time to time, I have more often than not been faced with people who have nut allergies. Particularly when running my Raw Happy stall at vegan fairs and markets all over the UK. I will generally use sunflower seeds as my go to raw cheeze, they are cheap, easy to buy, easy to digest and are high in vitamin E, which helps to keep our cardiovascular system strong and healthy.

My dear friend Helen Forester, who makes the most divine, high energy charged Malas you will ever see, I dedicate this recipe to you. I first met lovely Helen at Yoga Connects Festival in 2015, she was running her enchanting crystal and mala stall opposite my Raw Happy stall. As soon as I saw what she had on offer I knew my endless search for the perfect Mala was over. At the same time I knew my son Georgie would be totally made up to explore her high-energy crystals on offer and that we would both make a few purchases. Since that weekend of yoga and fun in the beautiful grounds of Stamford Hall, Helen and I have stayed in contact, seeing each other at other yogi events and even planning workshops together in the UK. Whenever I wear one of my beautiful mala necklaces or bracelets, yes I have a few. I can feel the love and positive energy Helen puts into her work and I always have someone comment on them and in turn usually purchase their own.

Check her out at www.chantmalas.co.uk

Ingredients
100g nuts or seeds of choice
¼ piece of yellow pepper
1 tbsp. apple cider vinegar
1 tbsp. Tamari
1 tbsp. Nutritional yeast
60ml or less of water
1 tsp. Probiotic
Nut bag or muslin cloth

Method
Start by soaking nuts or seeds and rinsing well before adding to blender with the other ingredients. Use as little water as possible just enough to get the blades moving and ingredients mixed well. Spoon mixture into nut bag and place in a large shallow bowl with a weight on top. Leave on the side overnight to ferment and for liquid to release, then remove from bag and put on plate in fridge to set. Ideally leave for a minimum of 24 hours, but the longer you leave the firmer your cheese will become.

Super Green Rockstar Pesto
This pesto was a creation by my group during the Rockstar Raw Food course in Richmond, London with Kate Magic. Kate has been an inspiration and fantastic guide to me throughout my plant based journey. Her company Raw Living

are my go to for any raw ingredients, from Kelp Noodles to Maca Powder. I highly recommend using this pesto on kelp noodles and perhaps adding Maca powder for an extra boost. If using the Maca add at the end after blending all the other ingredients, as it can taste bitter if over processed. Also consume the Maca pesto on the same day as making, because Maca can go 'off' quickly, again tasting unpleasant.

What is Kelp you may be wondering? Kelp is part of the seaweed family, which include Nori, Dulse, Sea Spaghetti, Arami and Kombu. There are many benefits to including sea vegetables in your daily diet, one in particular is their high iodine content, which is fabulous for healthy thyroid function. Our body is governed by our thyroid, having a thyroid which is out of balance can cause lots of unpleasant side effects and may result in imbalanced hormones and endocrine system.

For an added boost I have included sea algae in the pesto. You could use chlorella for a slightly milder taste or spirulina for a more powerful punch. Being a former mermaid I like to amp it up with a powerful heap of spirulina, but I always try to alternate the powders I use so my body doesn't become to complacent with a certain product. There are many different brands of green powders available now in health shops and online. Again do your research to check you are getting the best quality for your money.

Ingredients
30g Walnuts
70g Pumpkin seeds
1 clove of smoked garlic
1 date
1 tbsp. white miso
1 tbsp. Tamari
1 tbsp. Balsamic vinegar
125g Olive oil
Large bunch of mixed herbs- coriander, parsley, dill, basil
Add sea greens- Kelp, Chlorella or Spirulina

Method
Blend all the ingredients in a high power blender and serve inside wraps with cauliflower rice and salad, over sea spaghetti, zucchini noodles, or kelp noodles as suggested. Have fun experimenting with the herbs you use too, find your favourite combo or single flavour variation. Sweeteners are interchangeable too, if you are looking for a lower GI option try Yacon or Xylitol or omit the sweetener altogether.

Zuccini and Sesame Hummus

2 Zucchini peeled and chopped
2 tbsp. Sesame Seeds

1 tbsp. Tahini
2 cloves garlic
1 tsp. Tamari or ½ tsp. salt
1tsp. Apple Cider Vinegar
1 tsp. Cumin Powder
2 tsp. Baobab Powder

Add all ingredients to a blender and process and smooth

Creamy Red Ketchup
Who doesn't love dunking?! Exactly!!! Whether it be raw crudités or your favourite sweet potato wedges, then this healthy version of ketchup is for you! Regular shop brought tomato sauce has a super high sugar content, not friendly for your teeth and robbing your system of vital nutrients, minerals and vitamins. So enjoy this guilt free, tangy variation however you want. I like to add my Creamy Red Ketchup to my Mushroom burger recipe, with guacamole and hemp sour cream. Yum!!
Use this recipe as another way to get your superfoods in daily. Reishi is part of the medicinal mushroom family and loves to support your immune system. It is part of a group of highly potent mushrooms, which to name a few include Cordyceps, Lions Mane and Chaga, all serving us with a variety of healing properties. Medicinal mushrooms are strong in both healing qualities and flavour, therefore you only need to use in small amounts. A common misconception with superfoods is that they are expensive, however as you only need to use little and not so often you will find a pack can serve you over a long period of time.

Ingredients
60g soaked Goji berries
2 tbsp. Raw Tahini
Pinch of rock salt
1 tbsp. Apple cider vinegar
½ tsp. Reishi powder
2 tbsp. Olive Oil
Chilli flakes to taste
½ Red pepper

Method
Add all ingredients to blender and blend until smooth; add to your favourite spiralized noodles or for dips and accompaniments to your favourite dishes. You could also use this as a filling for Zucchini Roll Ups or as a layer in your lasagne.

Sushi Rolls
One of my favourite quick lunches or snacks. Nori rolls are nourishing, energising, light to eat, yet very satisfying. The

possibilities of fillings are endless, meaning you can eat them most days without getting bored. Below are suggestions of fillings, so try out different combinations and see which tantalises your taste buds the most.

Ingredients
Use up left over pesto, seed or nut cheese, mayo or ketchup
Fill with your favourite 'rice' using cauliflower, celeriac, parsnip, carrot or beetroot
Avocado
Carrot, Cucumber or Celery sticks
Sauerkraut
Spirulina, Chlorella powder
Fresh Mango
Umeboshi paste

Method
Take your nori sheet and place on clean surface with the lines running vertical, first use pesto, seed cheese or pastes. Smooth over the whole of your nori, leaving a small gap at the top, the end furthest away from you. Next spoon on your rice, not over filling, unless you want monster size wraps, yet making sure it goes right to the edges so once rolled you don't have empty ends! Finally put in any other fillings of your choice and now roll up your nori sheet. You can use bamboo rolling mats, but I just use my hands. Use water along the top edge to seal and press down firmly for a few seconds. The best tip I learnt for making sushi from my Teacher Kate Magic is to use scissors to cut your rolls. It really is magic too, so much easier than a knife. If you wanted to go traditional Japanese style use your chopsticks to dip in Tamari sauce and add a little wasabi paste on the side.

Walnut & Hemp Crackers
Ingredients
250g Walnuts
50g Hemp Seeds- with shells
150g Brown and Golden Linseed
50g Sunflower Seeds
1tbsp. Sumac
2tbsp. Tamari
2tbsp. Kombucha Vinegar
1250ml Water

Method
Soak walnuts and sunflower seeds together for around 4 hours. Soak hemp seeds over night in a separate bowl, rinse all nuts and seeds well keeping them separate. In a blender chop the walnuts and sunflower seeds, keep some texture to it, so don't over process. Add to a large bowl with hemp seeds and all remaining ingredients and combine together. Leave on the side for 4-6 hours until the linseeds have soaked up the water and the mixture has a 'jelly' element to it.

Spread evenly and not too thick on your dehydrator Teflex sheets and dehydrate for 12 hours. Flip off the Teflex onto the mesh sheets, score with a knife on the wet side into cracker shapes and dry for a further 8-12 hours until crunchy. Use to dunk in dips or sauces, with seed cheese, or as 'bread' for sandwiches.

Rapping Gangsta Wraps-

So these bosting raw wraps evolved from working on the vegan markets and fairs with my dearest friend and raw siStar Nafia Harding. Nafia and I met when I started teaching at Ella and Fleur Hot Yoga Studio in Cheltenham and she came to a class I was covering. From that first day we hit it off and a strong bond started to grow between us. Nafia was soon helping me out at festivals and even joined me on a raw food course with Kate Magic in London. Nafia had previously been running her own catering business, which has slowly evolved over the last year to be predominantly plant passed deliciousness too. I love working with Nafia as there is never a dull moment from start to finish the day will be filled with giggles, which makes all the hard work seem not taxing or stressful at all. A perfect example is one early morning as we were setting off for another vegan event, car was loaded and we set off from my place. As we pulled off my drive and along the road I was looking around thinking, 'It sounds really loud in here today'. Only to look back and see the boot was still wide open, but thankfully all of our food and market stall was still in place. Hahaha!! Love this girl and 2017 sees us starting venturing out to hosting and teaching and 'uncooking' on retreats in Devon.

Ingredients
Makes 6-8 large wraps or double crackers

Approximately 1.5kg or roughly 2-3 large bowls full of mix vegetables I like to use carrots, zucchini, spinach, kale, red peppers, and cauliflower
8-10 Sun dried Tomatoes
1 red onion
100g Sunflower seeds- soaked and dehydrated
1 tbsp. Cumin powder
1 tbsp. Coriander powder
2 tsp. Smoked paprika
2 tsp. garlic powder
1-2 tbsp. Tamari
1-2 tbsp. Apple Cider vinegar
500g Golden Flax seeds- milled to flour
1.5 litre Filtered Water

Process vegetables into small pieces, but again keep texture, not pulp. You could actually use veggie pulp left over from juicing but it would be a different consistency for the final wrap and crackers. This way they have more texture. Place vegetables in a large mixing bowl. In blender break down onion, tomatoes and then add to veggies. Finally in

PLANTALICIOUS: VEGAN RECIPES

blender break down sunflower seeds into smaller pieces but not too creamy we are still looking for texture. Add everything else along with sunflower and flax weeds to the vegetables and give it a good mix. Start adding filtered water slowly and stopping to mix occasionally. You want it to start binding and going glutinous. It will take about 1 to 1.5 litres of water. Spread out onto dehydrator sheets. For wraps dehydrate for 8-10 hours and then flip and dehydrate for a further 4-6 hours. For crackers once flipped, score into cracker shapes and dehydrate for a further 8-10 hours until crunchy. Play with different spices and herbs to find your favourite combination and taste.

Almond Marzipan Fudge
In need of a sweet treat then these are the perfect 'hit me up'! The beauty of making raw fudge is that the combination possibilities are endless. I honestly don't think I've made the same recipe twice. Try experimenting with different nuts and seeds too. Have fun!! Kids love to get making these with you in the kitchen. I've made them several times with Georgie and when I've been looking after my mate Lewis' daughter Grace too. Grace is actually one of my go to helpers, she assisted me on my kids workshop at Wholefoods Market Cheltenham. We also made these for a school coffee and cake morning in aid of a charity event. I was delighted we could offer a healthy option over sugar-laden cakes and biscuits, which were likely to be available and in my mind contradictory to the purpose of the fund raising purpose.

Ingredients
150g Almonds or pecans can work really well too
100g Coconut Chips
250g Soft Medjool Dates
1 dessert spoon Cacao Powder
1 dessert spoon Raw Almond Butter
1 teaspoon of Coconut Nectar or Raw Honey
1 dessert spoon Coconut Oil

Method
Blitz coconut chips in blender into a fine meal and remove 1/4 for rolling the fudge in at end, leave other 1/4 in blender. Add almonds and blitz before adding remaining ingredients and process until a dough ball is formed. Take out and with your hands roll into individual balls and roll in coconut. Keep them in the fridge.

Mulberry and Coconut Cupcakes
Ingredients for Cakes
150g Almonds
100g Mulberries
100g Coconut Chips
100g Dates
1tsp. Vanilla Powder

Method

Process the almonds, coconut chips and mulberries into fine flour. Add remaining ingredients and blend until dough begins to form. Take a small amount in your hands and roll into a ball, use bright or patterned cupcake cases and line a muffin tray. Press the ball into the case until it fits the case in a cake shape. Now make the topping

Ingredients for the Icing
1 Young Coconut Flesh
25g Cashews- previously soaked for 4 hours and rinsed well
75ml Coconut Water
50ml Coconut Nectar
2 tbsp. Coconut Oil
1 tbsp. Purple Corn Powder
3 drops Orange Essential Oil- doTerra Brand where available

Method

Blend all ingredients, apart from the oils, until smooth and creamy. Finally add the oils and blend again. Use a piping bag to decorate the cakes and add edible flowers.

Cantankerous Candidia Soup

This is my guest recipe from my most favourite place to eat in the world, the Seeds of Life restaurant in Ubud Bali. Every time I visit I feel so inspired, nourished and high on life it's unreal. When my friend Hannah McLaughlin came to visit me I took her there and she was blown away by Ben Richards, the owner's culinary creations too. I eat at other places in Ubud and then wish I'd gone to SOL, the cakes are extra special too!! Ben also boasts an in depth knowledge of Taoist herbs, which he offers in a very special Chinese tea bar in the café too. There are various concoctions to treat many ailments, offering healing on a deep level.

Ben posted this recipe on Facebook, with exceptional timing, as I was experiencing an invasive case of candida. When my body is low, from over exertion, my ecosystem becomes out of balance. Resulting in the levels of yeast dominating and causing unpleasant side effects such as bloating, exhaustion and brain fog. When I first became aware of candida I did a strong detox, eliminating a lot of high sugar foods and it helped to get my body back into balance. I now relate candida to high stress on my body rather than the foods I put into it. However if I do suffer with a bout of candida I do reduce my sweet intake of fruit, natural sweeteners and up the probiotics, Kombucha or Jun and greens to help get everything back to it's happy frequency and wave length.

Even if you are not experiencing Candida, this recipe is super delicious and nourishing so enjoy either way! And if you are in Ubud you 100% have to go dine at The Seeds of Life, for like breakfast, Lunch and dinner, oh and cake of course!

Ingredients for 1 serving
150mls Coconut Kefir
2 tbsp. Coconut Kefir Yoghurt- blend the flesh with kefir water and let it sit over night, blend again in the morning.

½ Avocado
1 Tomato
1 tbsp. Olive Oil
¼ cup Cucumber, no seeds
5 Sundried Tomatoes
5 Fresh Basil leaves, no stems
1 tsp. Fresh Oregano
½ tsp. Salt and Pepper
½ tsp. Chipotle Powder

Method
Add all ingredients to the blender and blend for 1 minute. Chop some fresh tomato and avocado chunks and add to the soup in a bowl. Sprinkle fresh chopped herbs over the top and serve with 1 piece of raw soft juicy onion.

I like to make an adaption of this recipe too, submitting the cucumber for zucchini, chipotle for a small red chili and the oregano for ginger, lemongrass and turmeric to create a Thai inspired dish.

Moussaka
I'm working on my book whilst in Gili Trawanagan, a small island off of Lombok in Indonesia. Quite often the case the electricity has cut out on the island, I'm told it doesn't happen as much as it used to and they are better at repairing it now. So my plan and motivation was to get up this morning, 21st December 2016 and work on my website. All was going well, the Internet had loaded quickly, I felt inspired to add new events and update my blog with news on my other new website, which is for promoting my retreats. Then the electric cut out, no stress, I got to work on other things such as retreat details for Bali 2017 and now onto writing more recipes and information in My Raw Food Journal. Sometimes we get caught up in routine, we had things in our head that should be done exactly here and now and as we had organised! Travelling in Asia has taught me it doe not always happen this way! The more we can learn to flow with the universe and embrace the unexpected occurrences the more we can enjoy and relax in our lives. I still sometimes get frustrated, but I am more able to now breathe, access and change or adapt. Taking time out to meditate each day has been a game changer, sometimes I feel more inspired thatn others to meditate, but even if I can spend 5 minutes to just be me in my body makes a huge difference. When was the last time you noticed your breathe, your life essence that is with you from the day you are born to the day we move on from this life?? Exactly, I know for years mine went unnoticed! Nearly everyday now I will practice Pranayama, or 'controlled breath.' Various breath work exercises where the breath is controlled rather than passive. I love taking time out to come home to my soul and be with my Prana, my life force energy. It can be healing, nourishing, energising and balancing. During my latest travels around Indonesia I have been blessed to practice my pranayama and meditation in such beautiful locations, on the beach with the waves lapping at the shore, in the jungle with the sound of insects and birds, behind powerful waterfalls. I have also been so grateful to share my knowledge with local people helping them to connect with their inner rhythms a little more. So realistically we may not always be able to find such magnificent locations or that much time, I know this is the case for me too when I'm in the UK. However even just finding time to be in nature for a

PLANTALICIOUS: VEGAN RECIPES

short while, or 5 minutes in the morning before rushing out the door on the school run or to work can make a massive difference to the way your day unfolds. Try it and let it develop and expand at its own pace.

Down to the recipe! This was one of the dishes I created for the opening night on Kashtat Bedu Bali 2016 retreat. I had made it in the uk also for an event, but having the opportunity to work with freshly picked vegetables off the side of a volcano was something special. Again if you do not have the means to dehydrating the aubergine I would suggest exchanging with zucchini, as raw aubergine is not so pleasant to eat. You could always swap the aubergine for nori sheets too, or even add them in as well as. The Moussaka tastes even better when it's slightly warmed, do this in your dehydrator for around 30 minutes or in an oven, which has been on and switched off with the door open until slightly heated through. Add this recipe to the Greek feast section if you re preparing a buffet or banquet for a dinner party or special occasion.

Ingredients for Aubergine
2 Small Aubergine
1 tbsp. Tamari
1 tbsp. Smoked Paprika
1 tbsp. Olive Oil
1 tsp. Agave

Method
Slice the aubergine thinly with a sharp knife or mandolin. In a large bowl coat the aubergine with all the other ingredients and leave to marinade for around 30 minutes. You could do this stage with the zucchini too if you are not using the dehydrated aubergine in the recipe. If using aubergine lay out individually on your Teflex sheets and dry high for one hour, then turn down to 41c and dry for a further 7 hours. Set aside while you prepare the other layers.

Ingredients for Tomato Layer
3 Red Peppers
6 Large Tomatoes
6-8 Sun Dried Tomatoes
4 Large Carrots
2 tbsp. Olive Oil
1 tbsp. Tamari
1 tbsp. Balsamic Vinegar
1 Date

Method
Chop all the vegetables into small pieces and add to your jug with the remaining ingredients. Process until smooth and set aside whilst you prepare the final layer.

Ingredients for the 'Cheeze' Layer
1 Small Celeriac, or if you can get 6 Jicama
100g Sunflower Seeds- soaked in advance for 4 hours
1 tbsp. Hemp Seed or Olive Oil
2 tbsp. Nutritional Yeast Flakes
1 tbsp. Physillium Husk
150ml Filtered Water

Method
Chop your celeriac or jicama into small pieces, drain and rinse sunflower seeds. Add both to blender with remaining ingredients apart from the Physillium husks and blend until smooth. Finally add the husks and process again.

Now you are ready to assemble the layers in a large Pyrex dish. Begin with the tomato layer, then aubergine, or zucchini or nori. Next a cheese layer, followed by aubergine or substitute. Tomato, aubergine and finally the cheeze layer on top. Now warm through before serving.

Mushroom Magic Burgers and Buns

Super Seeded Burgers
So many times I meet people at dinner parties or other raw food events who express their dislike of mushrooms. However once they try them raw it's a whole new ball game. One of my favourite and most simple ways to prepare mushrooms is to slice thinly and then marinade in the mixture listed below. I prepared some mushrooms like this when I was doing my yoga teacher training with Mercedes Sieff at her wellbeing retreat venue, Yeotown near to Barnstable in Devon. Least to say it was a massive hit!!
I can honestly say that the 3 weeks I spent on my Vinyasa Flow training with Mercedes, are in the top list of my best life experiences. I believe it was a significant turning point and milestone in guiding me towards my true-life purpose. Through a lot of self-inquiry and exploration I was able to start peeling back the layers from years of conditioning, misunderstanding and not truly being in touch with the real Tracy!! Starting to let go of these barriers and tune in with my heart, which allowed me to connect with the universal flow. Opening up the way for new opportunities and do what makes me happy and let my inner fire glow bright.

Ingredients
Makes 8 Burgers
1 Punnet Mushrooms- or save the stalks from the organic mushrooms for the bun.
300g Kale Leaves- Large Stalks removed
60g Shelled Hemp seeds
60g Sunflower Seeds
30g Golden Flax Seeds
¼ Red Onion

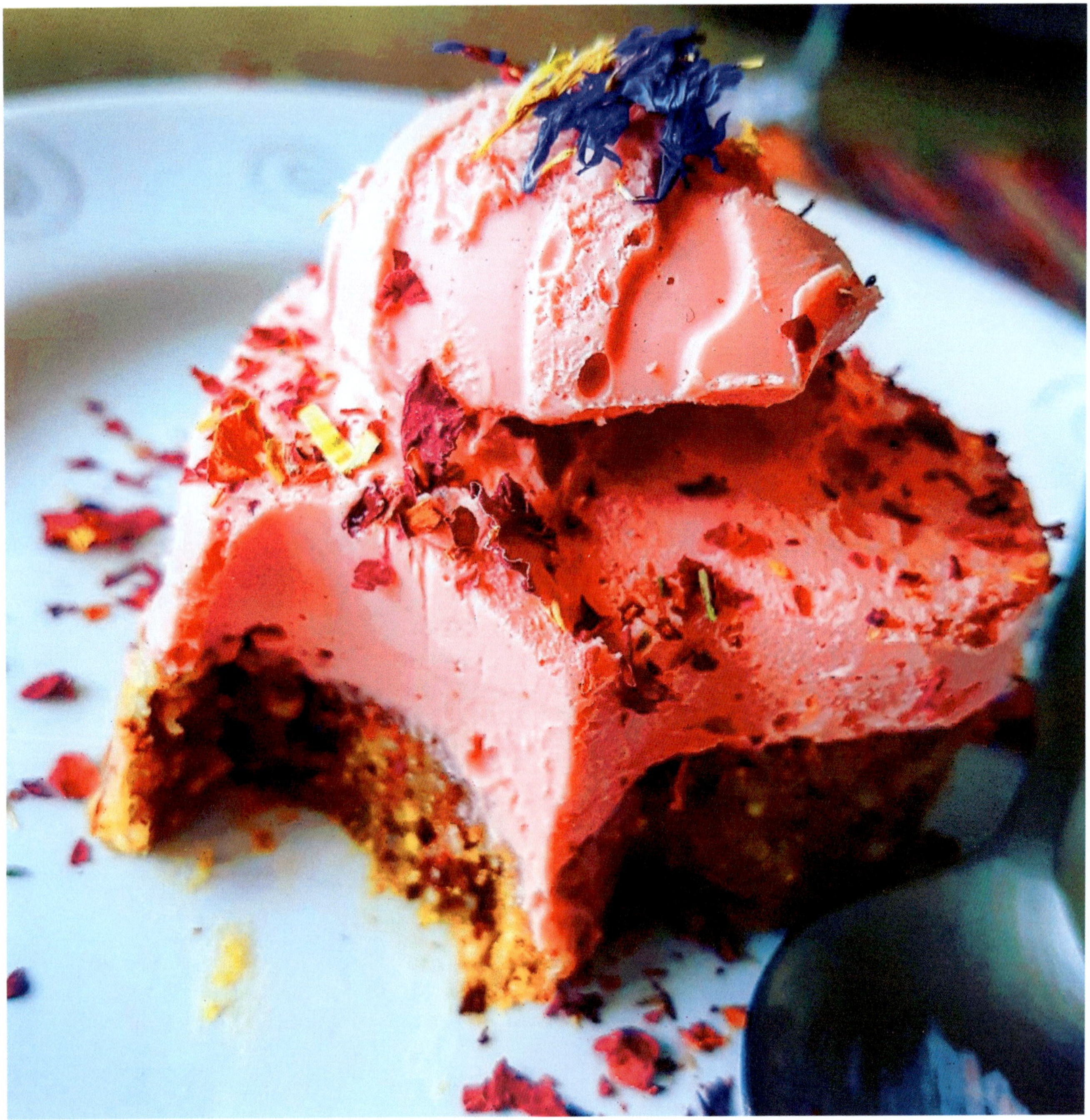

PLANTALICIOUS: VEGAN RECIPES

1 date
1tsp Balsamic Vinegar
1tbsp Olive Oil
Pinch Organic Rock Salt

Method
Grind Flax into a flour and set aside. In food processor break down mushrooms and kale, but keep texture, not too sloppy! Then add remaining ingredients and process. Transfer this mix to bowl with the flax and combine with fingers until it binds. Form into burger shapes with your hands and place on dehydrator sheets. Dehydrate for 8 hours turning halfway and removing form the Teflex sheet. Serve in crispy lettuce, in between Crackers or two large Portobello mushrooms with your favourite seed cheese, salsa and loads of leaves.

For the Mushroom Magic Buns
Ingredients
2 large Portobello mushrooms per serving
2 tbsp. Tamari
2 tbsp. Olive Oil
2 tbsp. Apple Cider Vinegar

Method
Remove stalks and outer skin from mushrooms or wipe outerskin with Veggi spray cleaner if they are organic. Combine other ingredients in a bowl and mix well before marinating the mushrooms for around 30 minutes. Once the mushrooms have absorbed most of the juices place on dehydrator trays and dehydrate for approximately 2-3 hours. They should just start to look a little 'cooked' and not get to dehydrated that they begin to shrivel. Fill as suggested above.

Dragonfruit and Coconut Cheesecake-
This was a creation founded on Kashtat Bedu Retreat Bali 2016. My plan had been to make a durian and coconut cheezecake, but with it not being local durian season, import fruits were up to 5 times the price!! In hindsight too, I think the durian may not have been to widely enjoyed by the group as this flavour was. The consistency is absolutely mega, really thick and creamy. Seek out dragon fruit in your specialist Asian supermarket or health shop, I can get them in Wholefoods Market Cheltenham where I do a lot of my workshops and events. However if you still can't find dragon fruit then substitute it with something easier to buy local to you, maybe mango or raspberry would work well.

Ingredients
Base-
100g Raw Coconut Chips
60g Hulled White Sesame Seeds
100g Lucuma Powder

1 tbsp. Coconut Nectar
2 tbsp. Coconut Oil
2-3tbsp. Filtered Water
Topping-
150g Raw Coconut Chips
1-2 Young Coconut Flesh
100ml Coconut Water
100g Cashew Nuts
90ml Coconut Nectar
100ml Coconut Oil
25ml Cacao Butter
1-2 Fresh Dragonfruit

Method
Grind the coconut chips and sesame seeds to a flour in your processor or blender, then add to a bowl with Lucuma and work with your finger tips to remove any lumps. Add remaining ingredients, apart from the water and mix well. Gradually add the water to bind, so just a little at a time and you may not need the full 3 tablespoons. Press the base firmly into your silicone mould or lined tin and set in the fridge whilst you make the topping.
For the topping place coconut chips in blender and process until a thick paste begins to form, this may take a couple of minutes. Soak cashews in advance, rinse well and add to blender with coconut water, coconut flesh, coconut nectar and process until smooth. Then add the Dragonfruit and blend until smooth, before finally adding the coconut oil and cacao butter and process again. I add the oils last to prevent them setting and sticking to the sides of the jug. Finally pour over your base, decorate as desired and set in the fridge or freezer.

Mango and Lime Cheesecake
This was one of my first cake combination creations and has proven a hit ever since. If I ever ask my son Georgie was cake to make for an event, his instant answer in 'Mango and Lime'. It's definitely a taste combination sensation. If you want to add a little spice, a small amount of chilli flakes in the topping works really well.

Ingredients
Base
100g Coconut chips
50g Goji Berries
60g Sesame Seeds
100g Lucuma
1 tbsp. Coconut Nectar
2 tbsp. Coconut oil
1 tbsp. Cinnamon
Pinch of salt

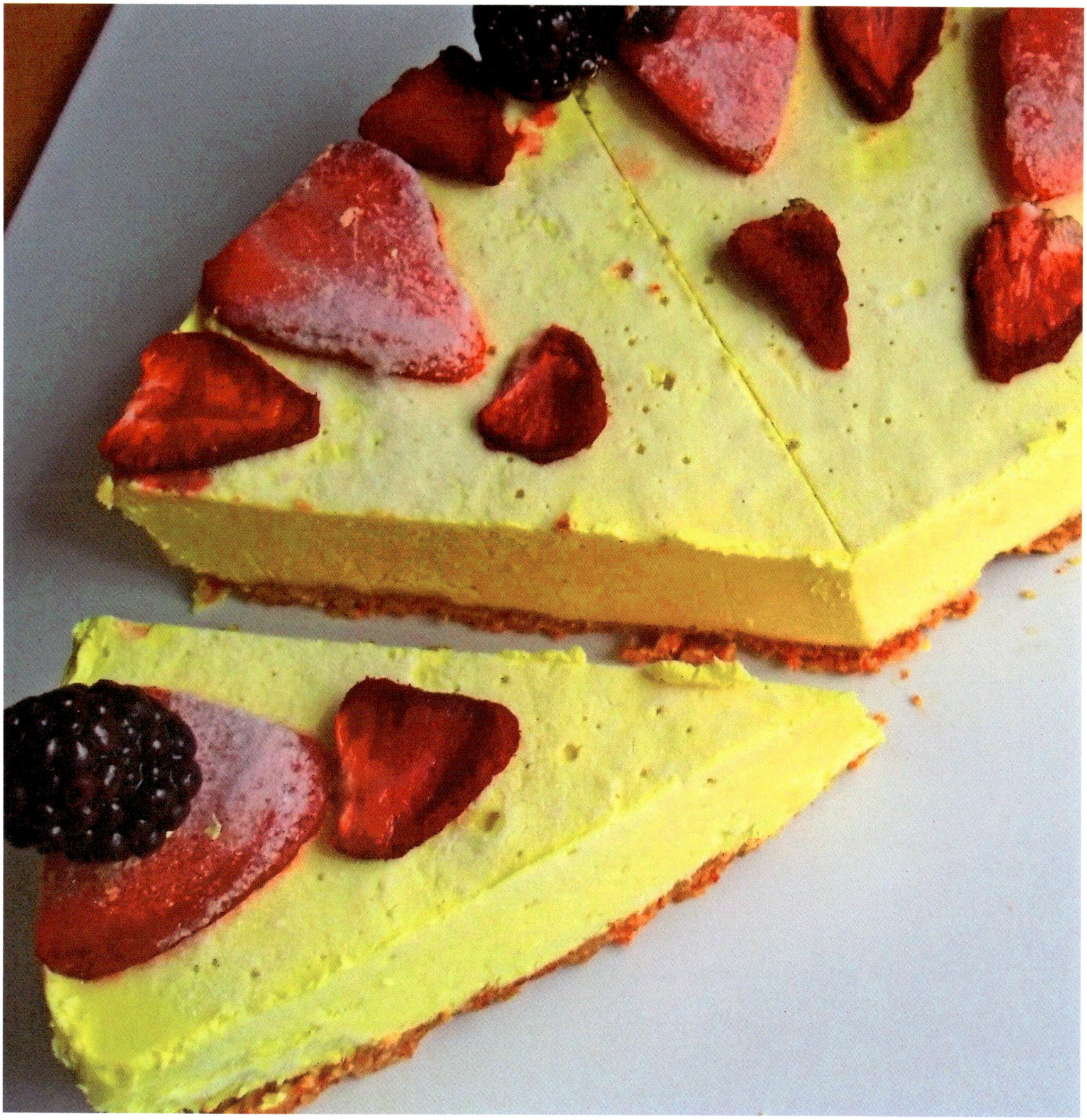

Grind coconut chips, goji berries and sesame seeds to a flour in your processor or blender, then move to a bowl with lucuma and work with your finger tips to remove any lumps. Add remaining ingredients and mix well, add 2-3 tbsp. of water to bind, not sloppy so just a little at a time. Press the base firmly into your silicone mould or lines tin and set in the fridge whilst you make the topping.

Topping
250g Cashews
1-2 Mango
1-2 Limes- flesh and juice, remove the rind
125ml Coconut oil
250ml Filtered water
1 tbsp. Turmeric powder
90ml Agave or Sweetener of choice

Add cashew and water to blender and process until smooth. Then add remaining ingredients apart from the coconut oil and process again. Finally add coconut oil and blend one more time, then pour over your base, decorate as desired and set in the fridge or freezer.

Krunchy Kale chips-

I'm certain kale chips were one of the first recipes I made in my dehydrator. There are infinite ways to make and enjoy these crisps. I often save the crumbs, if there are any, to sprinkle on other dishes, such as the raw lasagne. They give a delicious and nutritious crunch. A friend of mine once pointed out, that it's the crunchiness of food that we are addicted too. The more I thought about this and the more I observed patterns at my dinner parties and such events, I realised this to be true. There is certainly something comforting and moreish about that crunch and you won't get crunchier than Kale chips! My son Georgie loves this variation and if I say I'm making some he will always ask for them with the buckwheaties on as they totally make the kale chips extra special!

Ingredients
4-5 tbsp. Fennel, coriander or Caraway seeds
100g Spouted and activated Buckwheat
1-2 large bags of kale leaves approx. 250g
Sunflower seed Mayo- see recipe on page.

Method
Remove large stems from the kale leaves and tear into small pieces. Cover with sunflower seed mayo and massage really well to break down the leaf fibres, thus making the chips easier to digest. Sprinkle over the buckwheat and seeds of choice. Spread on Teflex sheets and dehydrate for 8-12 hours.

Buckwheat is a miracle food and contrary to belief, it is actually the seed of a flower and not a grain. It's a perfect alternative for those with allergies and intolerances as it is gluten free. Through tests it has been shown, that those consuming buckwheat in their diets, to significantly reduce cholesterol and lower blood pressure. It is a good source of magnesium, which supports the cardiovascular system and buckwheat is alkalising on the body too. Once you delve into the properties of buckwheat further, you will begin to discover its other amazing health benefits.

What is the difference between buckwheat and buckwheaties!!!?? To make your buckwheaties is a simple and beneficial process. The buckwheat seeds are soaked for 8 hours, to help break down the enzyme inhibitor and remove the gelatinous coating which can form. It is important to wash your seeds well after the initial 8 hours of soaking to remove this gel like consistency, which will form around the seeds. The soaking process will also remove any bitter taste from the final product. Once the seeds are well rinsed place them in your sprouter, this could even be a simple jam jar with a piece of muslin cloth over the end. The time it takes for your buckwheat to sprout will totally depend on the temperature, on warm sunny days in my kitchen the seeds will have sprouted their tails in a day. When the weather is a little cooler it can be up to two hours for them to sprout. Just be sure to rinse your seeds at least twice a day to help with the sprouting process. To tell when your buckwheat is ready check the small tail, which will begin to grow out of one of the pointed ends, this tail should reach no longer than the seed itself. Now your buckwheat seeds are sprouted, they are ready to dehydrate. If you are putting them straight onto your kale chips you do not need to dehydrate them first, just mix them in as directed and dehydrate altogether. Buckwheaties can be used in an array of sweet and savoury raw dishes as you will discover throughout My Raw Food Journal.

Almond and Cacao Energy Balls!
Almonds {1 cup}
Cacao {2 Tablespoons}
Medjool Dates {about 15}
Almond Butter {2 tablespoons}
Coconut Oil {1 Tablespoon}
Pinch of cinnamon if you want

In a food processor mix almonds first then all other ingredients, form into balls sprinkle with coconut and put them in the refrigerator.

Spicy Apple Slices
On a couple of occasions I have been inundated with copious amounts of apples and not known what to do with them. Thus evolved the beauty of the apple chip, although I'm certain others have made this discovery before me. The chilli in it satisfies my spice craving, so sometimes I can get a little over excited and add too much!! If you are not a fan of spice, simply omit the chilli flakes.

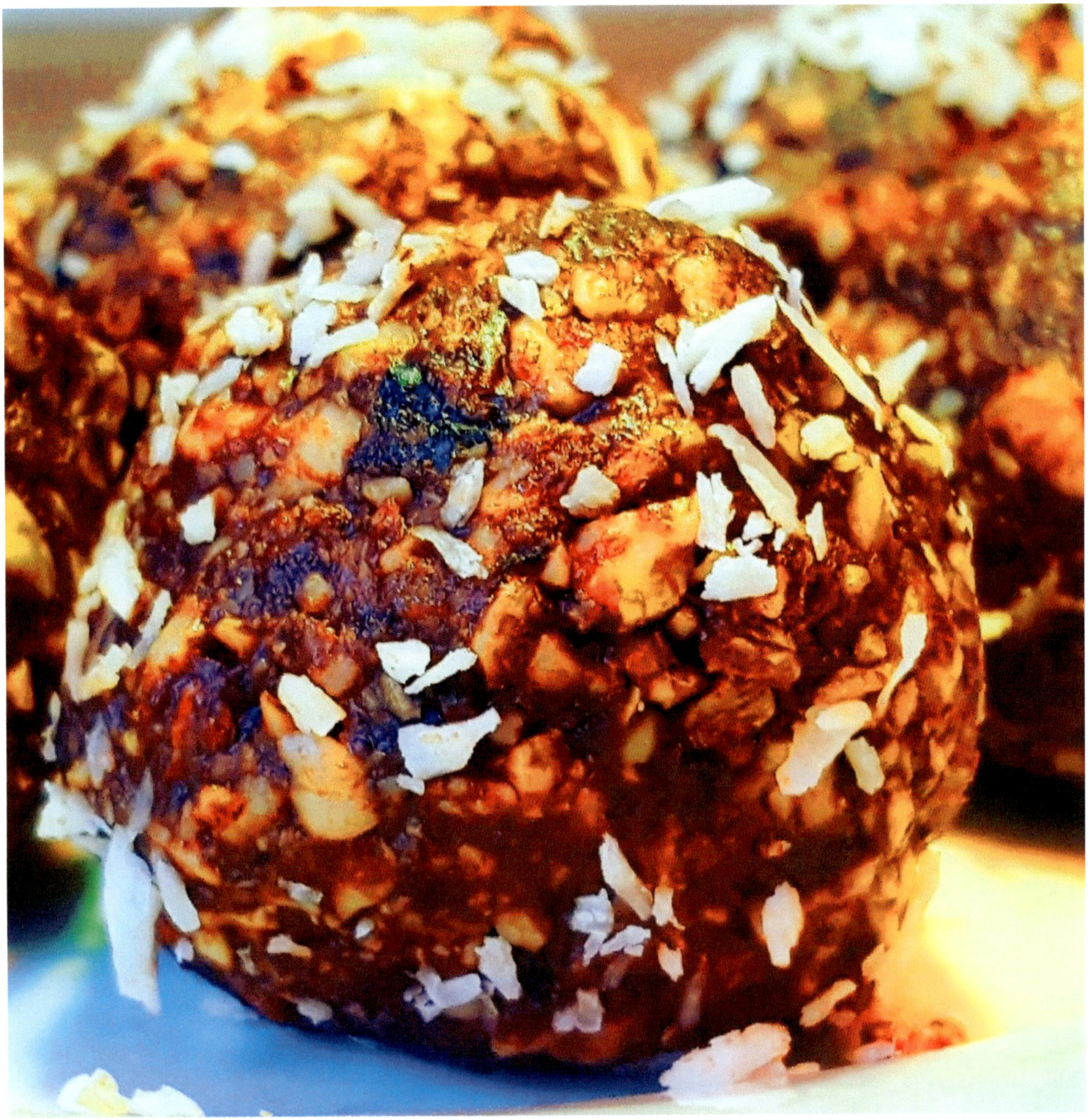

PLANTALICIOUS: VEGAN RECIPES

Ingredients
1 bag of your favourite Apples
3-4 tbsp. Apple cider vinegar- helps to prevent them turning brown
2 tsp. Cinnamon
1-2 tbsp. Coconut nectar
1 tsp. Chilli flakes
2 tbsp. Olive Oil

Method
Slice the apples super fine, if you have a mandolin use this. Then massage other ingredients in, covering completely. Spread onto trays and dehydrate up to 8 hours. A good substitute sometimes to use for a change in flavour is balsamic vinegar instead of apple cider.

Raw Salted Pecan Sauce
This is a delicious sauce that can be used on cakes, ice cream or even just fresh fruit.
1 cup pecans
1 cup pitted dates (medjoul)
4 tablespoons agave nectar
1 tsp sea salt

Soak the dates overnight and cover them with water. Drain the dates and save the water this date liquid will be used. Blend all ingredients till smooth and add date liquid 1 tablespoons at a time until the sauce is creamy. Drizzle over anything you want and enjoy!

Mini Apple Pies
I love making the pastry for the chicken pie and I sometimes make a raw quiche, so wanted to have a play with a sweet version. Apple pie is a real comfort food and this raw variation doesn't disappoint, with the combination of soft apple, creamy coconut and sweet seed pastry. If you do not have a dehydrator they will still taste yummy. You could even place them in a turned off, warm over for a while to heat up slightly.

Ingredients for the Pastry
150g Sunflower Seeds
100g Pumpkin Seeds
100g Golden Linseed
2 Dates
2-4 tbsp. Olive Oil
1tsp. Cinnamon

Method
Grind all seeds together to a flour. If you are using a food processor you can add the remaining ingredients and process to a dough. If you have a jug blender, you may find that too much mixture means it will not combine properly, therefore I bind it in two halves. Put dough on two Teflex sheets to roll out into large squares, you may have to add a little Lucuma on your rolling pin or cling film to stop the mixture sticking. If you are dehydrating, dry for 2 hours first, then cut into small even rectangular shapes before adding the filing.

Ingredients for Filling
Flesh from 1 Young Coconut
Coconut Water from the coconut
1-2 Apples
2tbsp. Coconut nectar
1 tsp. Vanilla

Method
Cut one apple into small chunks and coat well with coconut nectar, dehydrate for 4-6 hours until soft and 'cooked'. In your jug blender process remaining ingredients to a creamy puree. Now spoon a small amount of the coconut cream and a little of the cooked apples into the middle of each pastry bottom. Do not over fill or it will squeeze out of the sides when you press the top on. Carefully place the top over the filling and using a fork press around the edges to give a crimping effect to your mini apple pie. If the pastry isn't quite even, simply trim with a sharp knife. Enjoy like this or heat in the dehydrator for 2 hours.

Raw chocolate avocado cream cake

INGREDIENTS for the base:
17 dates (medjool)
1/2 cup ground almonds
1 tsp coconut oil

For the filling:
2 avocados
2 tbsp raw cacao powder
1 tbsp coconut oil
1/2 cup of coconut sugar
1 vanilla bean

INSTRUCTIONS

Mix the dates and the almonds and coconut oil in a food processor and blend until you get a dough. Put baking paper in a cake pan and put the base in first by pressing it into the pan. For the filling put everything else in a food processor and blend until its smooth, then pour onto the base. Put it in the freezer for about an hour then slice.

Durian and Coconut Cake-
Durian, the 'Marmite' of the fruits you either love it or hate it!! With its distinct flavour, texture and ultimately its unmistakable smell!! I've heard it described as smelling like 'gas' or fried onions, which may not make you want to rush out and buy some. In shops and airports over South East Asia there are even signs banning it on the premises, due to its pungent smell. Before my journey began on living foods, it was certainly something I didn't enjoy eating. My how times have changed along with my taste buds and now I cannot get enough of it!! When brought fresh Durian has a sweet delicious taste, with a creamy, almost avocado like consistency. Buying Durian in the UK has become easier over the last few years. Available frozen in Asian supermarkets and fresh when in season, some stockists even sell it freeze-dried. Combining the Durian with fresh young coconut meat makes this cake super creamy and satisfying! The topping can also be enjoyed as ice cream, as I discovered one evening when hosting a dinner party in Bali at my house with friends. The magic of the Durian fruit was singing out to us from the freezer, but it hadn't quite had enough time to set. Succumbing to the Durian charm we all enjoyed it more as a 'whippy' style soft scoop ice cream. One of the enjoyable parts of making this cake if you are using fresh durian is licking your fingers after! Again if the fruit is not available then substitute with something else, try banana and or avocado.

Ingredients
Makes 1 Small Cake
Base
100g Coconut chips
150g Dates
60g Sesame Seeds

In your high-speed blender blitz the coconut and sesame to a flour consistency. With a fork scrape the mixture from the corners of the jug, before adding the dates and blending again until the mix starts to bind a little. Again using the fork to scrape the mix out from the jug, press firming into the bottom of a silicone cake mould. Place in the fridge to set.

Topping or Ice Cream
Ingredients
1 Medium size Durian
Flesh from 2 Young Green Coconuts
100g Cashew Nuts
100ml Coconut Oil
50ml Cacao Butter

150ml Coconut Water- from the young coconuts
90g Coconut Sugar

Method
Pre-soak the cashews for 4 hours and rinse well, before adding to the blender with the Durian, Coconut flesh and Coconut water. Add the water gradually, as depending on the age of the coconut you may need less. The younger the coconut the less thick the 'meat' will be and the less water you will require. Once the mixture is blended down well to a cream add the sugar and blend again. Finally adding the coconut oil and cacao butter, I always add these last, if the other ingredients are too cold the oils will set to the sides of your jug. Pour over your cake base and set in the freezer for around 4 hours. Or if using as ice cream pour into a tub and set in the freezer, removing 10 minutes before you wish to enjoy to allow it so soften. Pouring a raw dark chocolate over and banana slices on top works well with this combination.

Carrot Cake
1 cup pitted dates I prefer medjool
1 tsp cinnamon
3-4 large carrots
Pinch of salt
1/2 Cup unsweetened shredded coconut
1 cup walnuts
1/2 tsp nutmeg

Cashew Cream icing
1 cup cashews soaked overnight
1/4 cup water
juice of 1/2 lemon
pinch of salt
1/3 cup oil
3 tbsp agave nectar
1 tsp vanilla

Instructions
Line a 9" pan with parchment paper in a food processor shred the carrots. Place in a bowl and set aside. Next blend together walnuts and dates until mostly smooth, with a few smaller chunks. Add coconut, spices, and salt and blend together. Add carrots and blend until well combined, scraping down the sides often

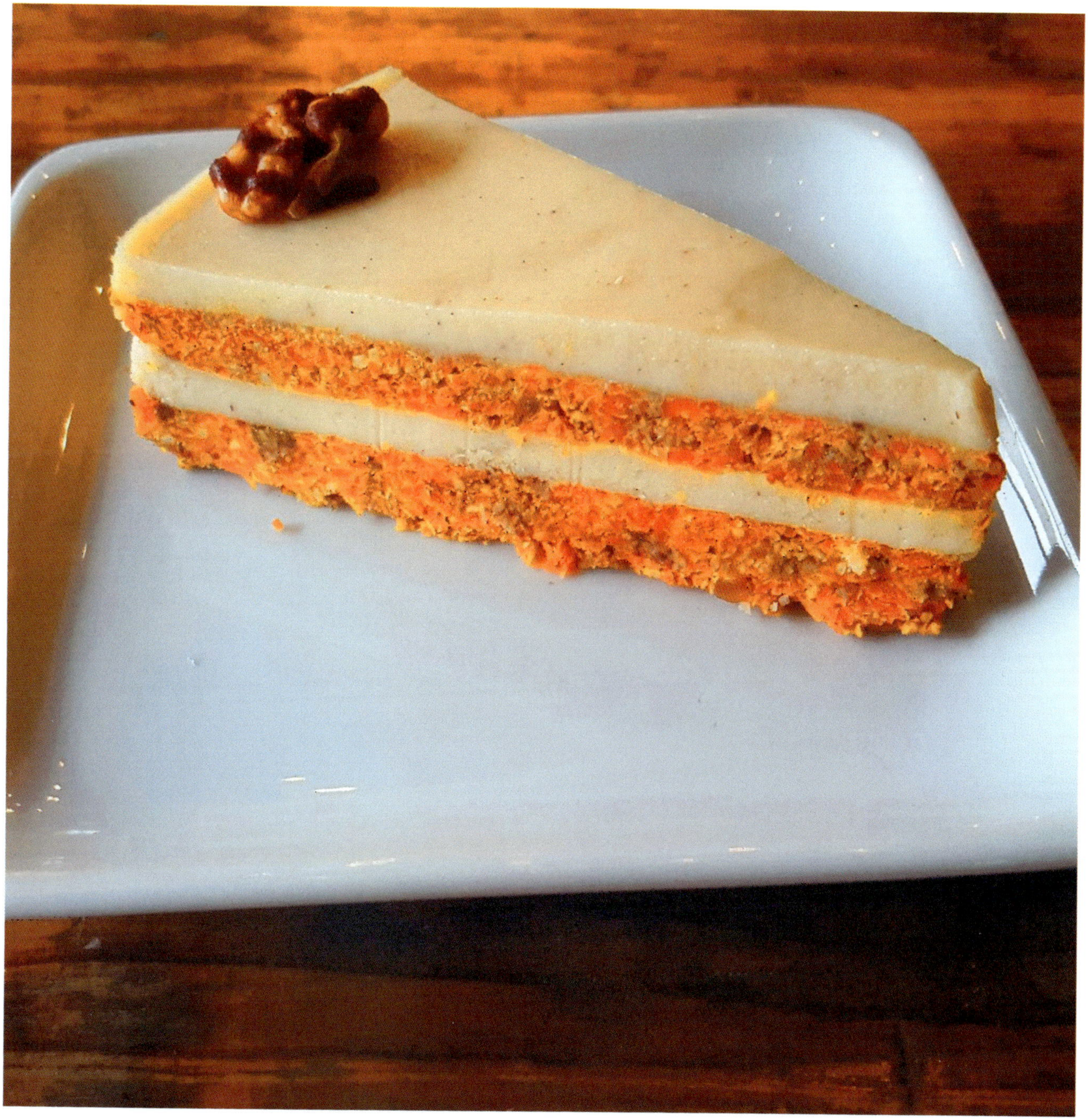

Scoop cake into prepared pan, smooth top, and put in the refrigerator To make cashew cream, drain and rinse soaked cashews in clean water. In a blender combine cashews, water, agave nectar, vanilla, salt, and lemon juice. Blend until smooth. Spoon onto chilled cake and smooth the top. Freeze for about 2 hours. Remove cake and Let thaw 10 minutes. With a hot, sharp knife cut cake. Decorate with walnuts and enjoy!

Carrot, Pistachio, Ginger and White Chocolate Cake
This was a new creation suggested by my dear friend and soul siStar, Hannah Burman. Hannah and I did our Angelic Reiki training together, going on a deep and transformational journey. The cake combination proved to be a winner for the awesome Soul Circus Festival in August 2016.

Ingredients for the Cake
250g Coconut Flour- made from milk pulp or blitzed coconut chips
100g Pistachio nuts
150g Carrots
150g Dates
1" piece Fresh Ginger

Method
Blitz coconut and pistachio to a flour and then blend with dates to form a loose dough. Grate ginger and carrots into a bowl, I like to use a hand grater or food processor for this, as when I use the blender it makes it too dry. Combine your flour dough with the carrot and ginger and press firmly into a silicone mould. Set in the fridge whilst making the chocolate topping.

Ingredients for Chocolate
150g Cacao Butter
50g Coconut Manna
100g Raw Honey or Agave

Method
Melt all of the ingredients together in a Bain Marie and then pour over your cake, decorating as desired, maybe with crushed nuts, grated ginger and Goji berries.

Goji Berry and Mulberry Chocolate Bark

Ingredients
1 Serving Raw Chocolate Recipe
25g Dried Goji Berries
25g Dried White, Black or Mixed Mulberries
1tbsp. Buckwheaties

1tsp. Dried Rose Petals- optional
3 drops of Rose Essential Oil- optional

Method
Make basic raw chocolate recipe as guided in recipe. Stir in remaining ingredients and spread on a baking tray lined with greaseproof paper. Set in the fridge or freezer. Again use this recipe to get creative and play with different dried fruit, dates and figs can work well. Perhaps substitute in different oils and edible flowers too.

Makes Everything OK Chocolate Cake
This is that ultimate chocolate fix that you can enjoy every minute of eating, without having to feel guilty about. So enjoy it as you nourish your mind, body and soul.
A really good friend of mine Jayne, who I met on my Vinyasa Flow yoga teacher training in Devon, asked me to make a cake for her wedding. There were a few vegan guests attending and a chocolate cake had been requested, so I was honoured with making such a creation.
I knew in my head what I wanted to make, but I was really busy with other events on the lead up to the wedding, so I allocated the day before Jayne and Matt's big day to get the cake made.
A couple of days before the wedding day, which was up in beautiful Cumbria, Jayne messaged to let me know there had been an incident with her other cake and that now mine would be the main cake for all the pictures!! UHHHH no pressure, especially when I hadn't even started it! I remember Jayne's message reading something like.. 'How's the cake coming along?' and me replying, 'Yeah it looks great in my mind!!' Haha!!

Anyways, the cake got made and my next concern was a four hour drive up North without the cake melting and arriving in one piece! Praise for the Thermobox and my 'Steady' (ahem) driving! The wedding started at 2pm and me and Georgie pulled into the car park at 1.45pm, saw a hotel steward, 'Where do I park please, I'm here for my friends wedding at 2pm', he looked at his watch, 'today or tomorrow?' Me, 'Today.' He was like, 'It starts in almost ten minutes', 'Yeah I know, where can I park and take the cake please?'

So got parked sharpish, quick change in the car from leggings to pretty dress, to the compliments of Georgie, 'Wow Mum that was a quick change!' No messing about here boy!
Running into the venue and placing the cake in a particularly hot room, please don't let it blooming melt now after safely transporting it all this way!
We were ushered to our seats, just in time for the gorgeous Jayne to make her appearance! Phew!!
What a beautiful wedding it was too, picturesque settings, late afternoon boat trip around the lake, dancing and chocolate cake. Jayne actually had to apply a fair bit of pressure to cut the cake, which she told me afterwards she was telling her new husband, Matt to press harder to get through! Ha!!
The cake is pretty dense with a lot of buckwheat and dried dates so no fear of melting! The icing can become a little soft, so I recommend keeping it in the fridge until you are ready to eat, if you can resist it that long! Have fun with this one.

TRACY SADLER & SYLVIA KENIMER

Ingredients
Cake
250g Dates- if they're hard soak them for 20 minutes in warm water
200g Coconut chips
100g Buckwheaties
100g Cacao Powder
1 tsp. Vanilla Powder
50-100ml Coconut water or milk
1 dessert spoon He Shu Wu- optional
1 dessert spoon Suma- optional

Method
Blitz coconut chips and buckwheaties into flour and set in large bowl. Add half of mixture back to the blender and mix with half the dates remove and do the same with remaining flour and dates. Put both parts into large bowl and add cacao powder, vanilla powder and other superfood powders if using with coconut water or milk. Gauge how much water or milk you need depending on the dryness of flour and dates. Mix well with hands, kneading and binding together and then press into your mould. As with the chocolates I like to use silicone moulds, as it's easy to get the cake out after. Set in fridge whilst making the icing.

Icing
1 Young coconut flesh and water
50g Shelled hemp seeds
50ml Maple syrup
50g Cacao powder
2 tbsp. Coconut oil
4 tbsp. Cacao Butter
1 dessert spoon purple corn powder- optional

Method
To make the icing place coconut flesh, seeds, syrup, cacao powder and purple corn powder, if using, into a blender and blitz until smooth, add coconut water a little at a time so that the mixture doesn't become too runny. Once smooth, add coconut oil and cacao butter and blend again until evenly mixed. If at this stage the mixture is too runny set in the fridge for 5-10 minutes until it starts to set slightly before smoothing over cake. Decorate as desired.

Raw Chocolate Brownies
1.5 cup walnuts
2.5 cups pitted dates
1/2 cup cocoa powder or raw cacao
1/2 tsp sea salt

1 tbsp maple syrup
1 tsp vanilla extract
1/2 cup dairy free chocolate chips or chopped dark chocolate

INSTRUCTIONS
Add the walnuts to a food processor or high-powered blender and blend then add the rest of the ingredients except for the chocolate until it forms a thick dough. Add the chocolate and blend Line a pan parchment paper or wax paper. Firmly press the dough into the pan. Put in the freezer for about an hour. Slice into 8 large brownies.

Cinnamon roll
This recipe was inspired by a trip to Sweden in 2016. I was on one of the small islands for a yoga retreat with the Rocketeer himself, Mr Lord Veda. It was a truly incredible week of twice daily yoga classes, hard-core Rocket practice in the morning and deep restorative Yin in the evening. I think one of the best phrases that came up during the week was "intense but casual", which has since been used to accurately describe certain events or situations. I met some super cool people and the group soon formed a close bond, feeling like we had all known each other before the retreat. For me it was a great break before the busy summer festival season and apart from enjoying lots of practicing yoga over teaching it, I got to put away my blender and enjoy lots of yummy creations by the talented Kimberley Parsons.
Sweden is a health and environmentally conscious country, super friendly, absolutely stunning and Stockholm boasts some of the best raw vegan restaurants I have eaten at. One of its national pastries is the cinnamon roll, which appear in most cafes, bakeries and shops. They're not vegan and definitely not raw, so I made it my mission to create a version which ticked both of these boxes. What a fun mission it was too. I love researching ideas, playing with flavours, ingredients and methods in the kitchen.

Ingredients
Pastry
150g Almonds
100g Pecans
150g Dates
75g Golden Flax Seeds
2-3 tbsp. Olive Oil
1tbsp. Cinnamon
1-2 tbsp. Water

Method
Process the flax seeds, almonds and pecans to resemble a flour consistency. Add dates, cinnamon and process again until a dough begins to form. Finally add the oil and gradually add the water. How much water you will require totally

depends on the softness of your dates. Spread your mixture out on the Teflex sheets of your dehydrator, dehydrate at 41C for 4-6 hours until its starts to firm a little, but without becoming too hard. Flip off the Teflex sheets and dehydrate for a further 2 hours before adding the filling.

Ingredients
Filling
60g Raisins
1 Young Coconut Flesh
50ml Young Coconut Water
1-2 tbsp. Shelled Hemp Seeds
1 tsp. Vanilla Powder
2tbsp. Chopped Pecans

Method
Blend the coconut flesh to a puree. Then add all remaining ingredients apart from the chopped pecans and a palm full of the raisins. Blend again to form a thick paste for the filling of your rolls. Spread over the pastry and scatter pecans and raisins, before rolling into a Swiss Roll shape. Using a sharp knife cut into small individual Cinnamon rolls approximately 1.5"-2" wide. Return to your dehydrator and continue to dry out for a further 2-3 hour, again just to firm up slightly, not to 'overcook'!

Earth Friendly Chicken Pie
Ingredients for Pastry
150g Almonds
100g Sunflower Seeds
1 tbsp. Miso- I like the Source Foods Organic brand
1tbsp. Raw Tahini
1-2 tbsp. Water
Method
Grind the almonds and sunflower seeds to a chunky flour consistency and then mix well with miso and tahini. You may not need the water and the mixture should be pliable not runny.

Filling
Ingredients
Flesh from 1 Young Coconut
1tbsp. Smoked Paprika
1tbsp. Tamari
1tbsp. Apple Cider Vinegar
1 tbsp. Sweetener of choice
1 portion of Maca Mayo

BLT

As I start writing this recipe I'm start in a local Warung (restaurant) on Kuta beach, Lombok. There was blaring techno booming out, whilst I'm overlooking the rural beach and hills. Not sure it's the ideal scenario, but then the music changes to reggae getting me more into my groove. Travelling isn't always the perfect picture you would envision, or expect. Seeing luxurious and beautiful places, relaxing, letting go of the stresses and strains of modern life. This is my first real trip to Lombok, an island north of Bali and it's taking a little while for me to adapt and settle in. It's a stunning, lush island, abundant with rice paddies, coconut palms and various other fruits and locally grown produce. Having just come from very touristy Bali and the Gili Isles, it was a shock to now see very few western tourists, all be that what I was wanting and expecting. I'm embracing the slower pace and quieter surroundings. I have also just realised this is my first time travelling alone, having previously always adventured with a boyfriend, child or friend, leaving me feeling a little uneasy. I think my greatest sense of unease comes from the large number of wild dogs patrolling the streets and beach. Having been bitten in Bali, by a pet dog, so thankfully no rabies, I've now lost my sense of ease with them previously experienced through all my years of travelling around South East Asia and around. Again meditate on these feelings, knowing that nothing is for ever and this is simply an emotion, or sensation I am feeling right now. It doesn't mean it will always be this way and that's ok. Life changes, it comes in and out with different circles, patterns, thoughts, emotions, sensations, it's all part of the motion of life. We are so led to believe that we should always be on the peaks and never the troughs, what crap! How would we experience the ecstasies if there was nothing to compare it too?

Well that was a bit devoid from this recipe, but relevant to my time of writing. A raw take on the 'classic' non-vegan friendly BLT, or bacon, lettuce and tomato sandwich. There's quite commonly the search for common connection with favourite or classic dishes, lasagne, shepherds pie, apple pie and so on. These connections bring about a sense of comfort, association and maybe happiness. I enjoy the creative element of making such a dish, which can be related to a meal or snack.

When making your bacon there are two methods I like to use, either with raw, dried coconut chips or fresh young coconut flesh. Both taste great and offer a different twist on the bacon filling for your sarnie, so maybe have a play with both varieties and see which hits the spot.

Ingredients
Raw Bread or raw crackers or Sprouted Bread (not raw) I like the Everfresh Bakery brand
Rocket leaves
Tomato Relish- Use Tomato Ketchup recipe, omit the tahini and red pepper. Try using tomato and adding physalis, golden berries or fresh root ginger for an added punch.
Sunflower Seed Mayo- Use the Maca Mayo recipe, for a milder less dominating flavour, simply omit the Maca powder.

Coconut Bacon
Ingredients
100g Dried Coconut Chips or 1 Fresh Young Coconut
1tbsp. Smoked Paprika
1tbsp. Tamari
1tsp. Balsamic Vinegar

Method
In a bowl thoroughly coat your coconut and then spread evenly over your Teflex sheets. Dehydrate until completely dry, around 6 hours. These will keep in an airtight container in the fridge for 1-2 weeks.
To assemble your sandwich, take two slices of bread of crackers, spreading one with sunflower seed mayo and the other with tomato relish. You can add extra slices of fresh tomato along with the rocket, or other leaves if you prefer. Add a good spoonful of your coconut bacon and close two halves of the bread together. Enjoy with dehydrated crisps, fresh leaves a yummy kale salad. If having kale, keep it simple, massaged lovingly, yet thoroughly to break down the fibres, in fresh lemon juice and rock salt.

Basic Chocolate and Filled chocolates
I never really used to be a fan of chocolate, that was until I discovered raw cacao, now I probably have a little most days. Its health properties are literally off the scale on the ORAC (Oxygen Radical Absorbance Capacity) meter. The ORAC scale is used to measure naturally occurring antioxidants in food, with blueberries and broccoli fairing high up on the scale too.
Raw, unspoilt, natural chocolate is abundant in iron, zinc, calcium and magnesium, common deficiencies in western society, due to depleted soils from over farming. Unlike chocolate with added dairy, which inhibits the absorption of cacao's natural benefits, raw cacao can aid in having a healthy heart, balance hormones, make you feel happy and assist in combating depression and is naturally high in antioxidants.
Have respect for mother cacao too, as a little goes a long way and indulging in too much can put stress on your adrenals and be a cause for fatigue. Although if used accordingly cacao can help to combat fatigue.

A recent craze is cacao ceremonies, which actually date back to ancient Aztec and Mayan civilisations and their use of cacao to praise the gods during rituals. The retreat I ran with my friend Katie Holland in Bali 2016, saw our lucky guests experiencing such a ceremony. It was extremely healing and brought about a sense of euphoria and the ability to let go of the old and bring in the new. A lot of tears were shed by all as we succumb to the power of this sacred plant and connected with our inner and higher selves. Once you have the basics of cacao making you can start to play with a variety of fillings and flavours. I love to use essential oils in my chocolates for an extra special touch, sometimes lavender or orange. When using essential oils, be sure to check that they are food grade and organic. My go to brand is doTerra, who offer an amazing variety and top grade quality.
So now you don't have to make up excuses for your love affair with the chocolaty good stuff! Enjoy!!

Basic Raw Chocolate
Ingredients
150g Cacao Butter
100g Cacao Powder
50g Yacon Syrup or Sweetener of choice
100g Yacon Flour or Lucuma

Method
Melt cacao butter and sweetener in a Bain Marie, make sure the water is not boiling as you will loose the raw properties of the ingredients. I recommend melting the sweetener and cacao together to avoid 'splitting' or separation once poured into the moulds, I also find that blending them lightly together helps to prevent this also. It should take approximately 10 minutes for the cacao to melt. Blend cacao butter and syrup with cacao powder and Lucuma, pour into moulds. Stir oil in at the end if you are using.

Filled Chocolates
Ingredients
Raw chocolate recipe, as above
1 dessert spoon Raw Tahini or you're favourite Nut butter
1 dessert spoon Sweetener- coconut nectar
1 tsp. Coconut oil
1 tsp. Yacon flour or Lucuma
Water if needed

To make the filling, mix all ingredients apart from the raw chocolate in a small bowl. You may or may not need the water, you want the mixture to be more like a paste than overly runny. Pour the raw chocolate into the silicone moulds, half filling. Add a small amount of the filling in the centre of the moulds and then pour more chocolate to cover and fill the mould. Set in fridge or freezer.

Hemp and Banana Maca Smoothie
In need of an energizing start to your day, refuelling after a good workout or yoga session, then this is the bad boy for you!! Hemp is a wonder plant in so many ways, other than nutritional benefits, it's a super strong building material, grows really fast making it much more environmentally friendly. Cool fact, a tree can take up to 50 years to grow and be ready to be harvested for building material, but hemp takes a mere four months!! Time to change our game plan me thinks! Hemp is full of good fats, EFA's (essential fatty acids), it's a complete protein food containing all the nutrition we need. Our cells require these minerals as building blocks for, good memory, and healthy joints. It can also reduce illness and inflammation in the body, so enjoy this smoothie knowing that you are doing so much good for your beautiful body and the planet.

Ingredients
1 tbsp. Shelled Hemp Seeds
1-2 Frozen Banana
150ml Water or Coconut Water
1tsp. Raw Honey or 1 Date
1tsp. Maca Powder

Method
When freezing your banana, peel and chop into small pieces first. In your high speed blender process the hemp seeds, banana, water and honey to form a smoothie consistency. Finally add the maca, to be sure not to over process and turn the flavour bitter.

Green Juice
Ingredients
1 cucumber
3-4 stalks of celery
2" piece of ginger
Small piece of fresh turmeric root
1 lemon, lime or ½ grapefruit
Dark green leafy vegetables- spinach, kale, Cavolo Nero

Method
Run all the ingredients through your juicer or if you cant face washing the juicer out after- quite often my case. I blend all the ingredients and then squeeze through my nut bag. Much easier!!

If you are susceptible to thyroid issues please be careful with over use of green vegetables in your juice as this can affect your thyroid over time. You can still follow the recipe as above but just leave out the greens, maybe add spirulina or chlorella powder instead after juicing.

White Chocolate and Macadamia Cupcakes
Ingredients for Base
150g Mulberries
100g Macadamia Nuts
100g Dates

Method
Process nuts into small pieces and then add mulberries and dates to combine. It should still have texture and not become a paste. Press firmly into your cupcake moulds, again I find silicone are the easiest to work with.

Ingredients for the Middle
Macadamia Nuts
1x Young Coconut Flesh
1-3 tbsp Water
2tbsp. Agave Nectar
2tbsp. Cacao Butter

Method
Macadamia are one of the nuts which do not need soaking, same as pecans and pistachios. Start by melting your cacao butter, whilst preparing the other ingredients. Add the nuts along with coconut flesh, water and nectar. Process until smooth and creamy and finally add meted cacao butter and blend again. Pour over the base leaving enough room at the top for the white chocolate layer.

Ingredients for the Topping
100g Cacao Butter
50g Coconut Manna
50g Coconut Oil
75g Yacon Syrup

Method
Melt cacao butter with other ingredients and then blend together in the blender until well mixed and smooth. Pour into moulds and set in the fridge or freezer. If adding decoration allow the topping to set a little first so that the decoration does not sink.

Greek Feast.
Falafel
Ingredients
100g Activated Sunflower Seeds
100g Activated Pumpkin Seeds
15-20 Sundried Tomatoes
1 Desert Spoon Cumin Powder
1 Desert Spoon Smoked Paprika
1 Desert Spoon Tamari
Small Bunch of Fresh Coriander

Method
Combine all ingredients in your blender or food processor. The mixture should still have texture and not be over processed to a paste. Using a fork remove small amounts and roll into balls. The falafel can be enjoyed like this or dehydrated for around 4-6 hours. Serve with Tabbouleh, Tzatziki and Fresh Greek Style salad.

Tzatziki
Ingredients
250ml Coconut Kefir
1 Young Coconut Flesh
½ Cucumber
Small Bunch Mint

Small Bunch Dill
1 tbsp. Olive Oil
½ tsp. Salt

Method
In blender combine the coconut Kefir and flesh with oil and salt. Cut the cucumber by hand into small cubes, removing the inner seeds, as this is the wettest part of the cucumber and will cause your dip to go watery. Add to a bowl with the chopped mint, dill and coconut mixture. Combine all together by hand and serve with Tabouleh, Falafel and Greek Style Salad.

Tabouleh
Ingredients
1 small Celeriac, or if you can get it 2-3 Jicama
Small bunch of Parsley
2 Large Tomato's
½ Cucumber
2-3 tbsp. Hemp Seed Oil
2 tbsp. Shelled Hemp Seeds
2 tbsp. Hulled Sesame Seeds
1tbsp. Apple Cider Vinegar
1 tbsp. Tamari

Method
Process the celeriac or Jicama into 'rice' size pieces either by hand, in the food processor or blender. If using a blender, use it on a number 2 or 3 so it doesn't turn to mush. Chop the tomatoes and cucumber into small pieces and finely chop the parsley. Put all ingredients in a large bowl and mix carefully with your hands, putting good intention into your food. Enjoy with your other Greek feast dishes.

Grawnola
Ingredients
150g Buckwheaties
2 Apples
5 Pears
8 Dates
25g Goji Berries
25g White Mulberries
8 Dried Figs
2tsp. Cinnamon
1tsp. Nutmeg

Method

If your apples and pears are not organic then peel them, otherwise keep on the skin and then chop into small pieces to fit in your blender and process to a puree. I find it's easiest to use scissors to finely chop the dried fruits into small pieces. In a large bowl place all the ingredients and mix until well combined. Spread mixture out evenly onto your dehydrator sheets and dry on high for one hour, before turning down to 41C. This is quite a wet mixture so will take at least 24 hours of dehydrating. I dry for at least 15 hours before flipping off the Teflex and dehydrating for up to another 8-9 hours. It should be totally moisture free and chewy slightly. Once your grawnola is ready cut or tear into small pieces and store in an airtight container, where it will keep for at least 2 months. Enjoy with your favourite nut or seed milk.

Vanilla Hemp Filling
Ingredients
50g Shelled Hemp Seeds
1 Young Coconut Flesh
80ml Coconut Milk or Water
2tbsp. Agave Nectar
1tbsp. Lemon Juice
½ tsp. Vanilla Powder

Method
Add all ingredients to your high power blender and process to a smooth cream. You may need less or more coconut water or milk again depending on the age of your coconut and how thick the flesh is. If using coconut milk then try making your own, it's so simple and tastes totally awesome. Using brown coconut flesh, chop into small pieces and add to your blender with enough filtered water to just cover the coconut. Blend and then strain through your nut bag, the milk will keep for up to 2 days in the fridge and you can use the desiccated coconut for other cake recipes. I love using my Love Tree Products nut bag as they're organic cotton or organic hemp. Head to https://www.lovetreeproducts.com/en/ to buy yours.

Zucchini Fries
I remember the first time I made these was for a private dinner party at my yoga teacher's house. I love hosting dinner parties, it's a chance to play with new recipes and come together with a group of generally like-minded people. Sometimes the guests may never have tried gourmet raw foods before, so it can be a new experience and real 'eye opener'. The most common feedback after first trying raw, or living foods is, 'Wow the flavours are so intense"! A common misconception of eating a plant-based diet is that we are really deprived of tasty food, this couldn't be further from the truth. Raw vegan food is probably the most taste tantalising foods I have ever experienced.
This recipe was one of those Tracy moments of seeing what spices I had in the cupboard and 'chucking' it in! So as I always say, feel free to experiment and find your own favourite flavour or combo.

Ingredients
4 Zucchini
1tbsp. Chinese Five Spice
1tbsp. Olive Oil

Method
You can either slice with a knife into fries, or use your mandolin to slice into thin circles. The circles will give you more of a crisp than a chip. Coat your fries or crisps with the spice and oil and massage well to make sure fully coated. Spread evenly on your Teflex sheets and dehydrate on full for 1 hour and then turn down and dry for a further 4-6 hours if you're making fries and up to 12 hours if you're making the chips. It's delicious to experiment with other vegetables too, perhaps sweet potatoes or beetroot as chips and carrots as fries. If you can find Jicama then these make delicious fries also. I've not found jicama outside of Indonesia yet, but it's super yummy. They look like a potato, have an apple texture and are really juicy, they make a great substitute for 'cauliflower' rice too.

Cherry Chocolates
These were a hit at one of Jayne's Devon yoga retreats, I even had a request to make some for a returning guest on the following retreat. You could try them with various dried fruits inside, but there is definitely a special alchemy of the sourness of the dried cherry with the smooth, bitter tasting raw chocolate. Gosh I'm getting a craving writing this recipe and I'm currently sat in East Lombok where there is no sight of raw chocolate whatsoever!! Arghhhhh Help!!
I use the liquor in this recipe because it has a thicker consistency that works well with the coconut oil to resemble a chocolate ganache. I remember sitting with my dearest friend Shaye in one of our favourite raw vegan jaunts in London, where we tried this amazing cake with this divine chocolate ganache topping. 'Shaye, I gotta go recreate this!!!'

Ingredients
150g Cacao Liquor
75g Coconut Oil
100ml Yacon Syrup
2tsp. Lecithin Granules
Dried Sour Cherries

Method
In a Bain Marie melt cacao liquor and coconut oil with Yacon syrup and then blend on a low speed with the lecithin. Using the lecithin will make the chocolate super smooth and creamy. Pour the chocolate mix into your moulds, but not quite to the top so that you can push your cherry into the middle without it over flowing. Using the cacao liquor will make the mixture generally thicker to start with, so you will need to work quicker to avoid it setting to fast.

Walnut and Pecan Donuts with Carob Icing
Ingredients for Donut
150g Pecans
150g Walnuts
150g Dates
100g Cacao or Carob Powder

Method
Process nuts in to flour and then add remaining ingredients to form a sticky dough. Press into your donut mould, I use my silicone one as it's easy to remove the donut once you have formed the shape. If you do not have a mould, simply shape by hand.

Ingredients for Icing
2 tbsp. Tahini
2tbsp. Carob Powder
2tbsp. Coconut oil
2tbsp. Agave

Method
In a bowl mix all ingredients together and then smooth on top of your donuts. Remove donut from the mould before icing to make it easier, Decorate with goji berries and bee pollen.

Nommytella
Ingredients
200g Hazelnuts
150g Cacao Powder
100g Coconut Nectar
50ml Fresh Coconut Milk

Method
Firstly make your coconut milk as per the basic nut milk recipe, remembering to keep the pulp for cake recipes. To make the Nommytella in your jug process all the other ingredients along with your fresh coconut milk. Keep in an airtight jar in the fridge for 1 week. It tastes great on raw crackers, breads, or use for a cake topping too.

Twix
Ingredients for Base
150g Buckwheaties
50g Cacao Nibs
100g Yacon Flour or Lucuma
75g Yacon Syrup or Agave
1tbsp. Water

Method
In a bowl mix ingredients together so they stick, add the water a little at a time. Roll between your hands to make a sausage shape and square off the ends. Dry for 4 hours.

Ingredients for Toffee
100g Dates
50g Lucuma
1tbsp. Maca

Method
Blend all ingredients together to forma a toffee. Spread over the base and set in the fridge while you make the chocolate topping.

Ingredients for the chocolate
Follow the basic chocolate recipe

Method
Let the chocolate cool a little before you pour over the bars, this way it wont run off the bars and will stick. Set in the fridge.

Balinese Green Pancakes
In October 2016 I hosted my first international retreat in Bali with my friend Katie. We had 8 lovely guests join us for 10 days of spiritual dance, yoga, meditation, living food and adventures around the island. One of the favourite breakfasts was a Balinese style pancake, which were vegan and gluten free, obviously my mission was to recreate a raw version!! Mission accepted and completed.

Ingredients
250g Coconut flour or left over milk pulp
150g Chia flour made by grinding chia seeds
100g Coconut Nectar
2tbsp. Spirulina or Moringa Powder
250ml Water

Method
Mix all ingredients together and then form into thin round pancakes on your Teflex sheets. Dehydrate for 8 hours and then flip onto mesh for a further 4-6 hours. Fill with fresh banana, grated fresh coconut and coconut nectar.

Papaya, Banana and Tahini Ice Cream
So what do you do with left over bits of fruit or over ripe bananas, you make the best ice cream ever, that's what! No nasties, just wholesome nutritious goodness with fruit and superfoods. Feel free to have a play with this recipe by substituting the tahini for a nut or seed butter of your choice. You can even begin to make it a little 'fancier' by adding in or using cashew nuts or hemp seeds. Sometimes though simplicity is best.

As I'm writing this recipe, there has been a power cut at the guesthouse where I'm staying, in East Lombok. It's 7pm and as my laptop screen is currently the only light source, I seem to have attracted every insect in town and I'm now being bombarded with hundreds of bugs and flying insects! Hahah!! I was actually meant to leave the island today, but Lombok is magical and has wooed me to stay a little longer. My current abode is at the foot of Rinjani Volcano, the second largest volcano in Indonesia. Many tourists come to trek the mountain and visit the crater, lake and summit, taking up 2 days and 3 nights. I plan to return in 2017 to partake in the majesty of Mount Rinjani. Read more about my precious time spent in Lombok in my local ginger and coconut sweets recipe

Ingredients
2 Frozen Banana
½ Frozen Papaya
1tbsp. Tahini
2tbsp. Lucuma

Method
Super simple. Just add the ingredients to your blender and whizz to a thick soft scoop consistency. You may need to add a little water to help the blades move. Serve sprinkled with buckwheaties, goji berries or any of your other favourite toppings.

Jeje Jae Sweets
These delish ginger and coconut sweets are from Tetebatu in Lombok. It was a great discovery tasting these sweets from my family in Lombok and best of all they're raw too! Just 3 simple ingredients and you will be in taste heaven. It was actually quite a funny scenario, as I'd just made a raw cake, with very basic and simple ingredients that I could get in this remote part of east Lombok. So while the family enjoyed my creations I enjoyed theirs!

Ingredients
20g Fresh Grated Ginger
200g Fresh Grated Brown (old one) Coconut Flesh
75g Coconut Palm Nectar

Method
Simply combine all of the ingredients in a bowl and mould together. Press into small squares and enjoy like this or dehydrate for a few hours.

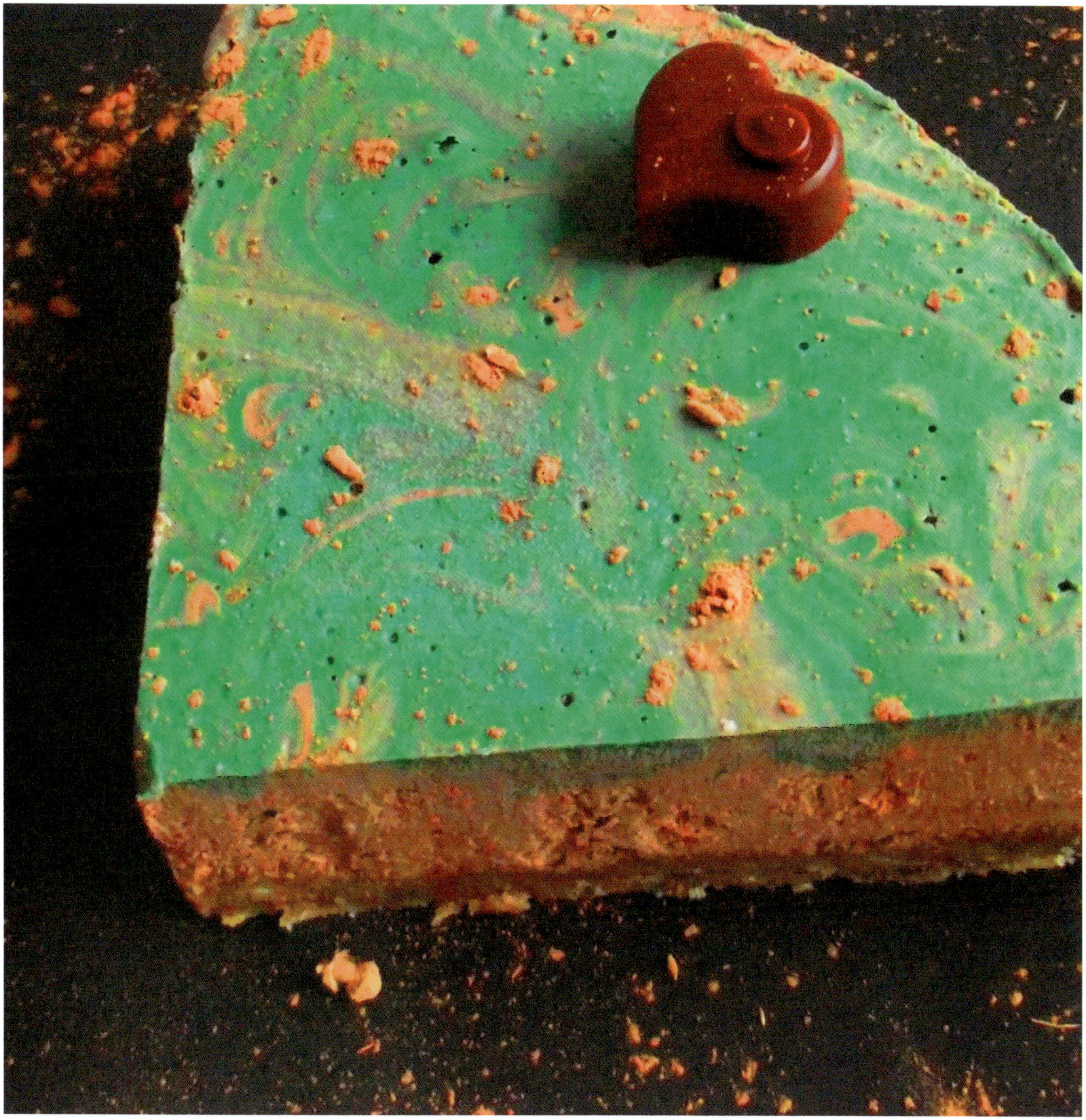

Chocolate and Mint Swirl Cake

Base
100g Pecans
150g Walnuts
100g Carob Powder
75g Coconut Oil
2tbsp. Agave

Method
To make the base, process the pecans and the walnuts separately to avoid the mix clumping together. These nuts contain a lot of lovely natural oils and if over processed with turn into nut butter very quickly. Which is yummy and fab, but not quite what we are after in this recipe. In a bowl mix the broken down nuts with other ingredients and mix well. Press firmly into a cake mould using either a spatula or back of a wooden spoon. If you find the mixture sticks, slightly wet the utensil.

Mint Layer
1x Young Coconut Flesh
1tbsp. Spirulina
4 drops Food Grade Mint Essential Oil
50g Coconut Oil
20g Irish Moss- soaked and rinsed
100ml Water

Method
Prepare the Irish moss as explained in the methods section of this book. Add the well-rinsed moss with the water to your blender and process on high until the fibres are broken down. Scrape the coconut flesh (keep the water, you might need it for the chocolate layer) into the blender jug along with Spirulina and mint essential oil- check the oil you are using is food grade. I recommend doTerra oils for culinary use. Blend until smooth and finally add in the coconut oil for the last mix. Set this aside whilst you prepare the chocolate layer.

Chocolate Layer
1x Young Coconut Flesh
100g Cashew- soaked for 4 hours
75g Agave
75ml Coconut Oil
20g Irish Moss
2tbsp. Lecithin
50g Cacao Liquor

Method
Prepare the Irish moss as explained in the methods section of this book. Add the well-rinsed moss with the water to your blender and process on high until the fibres are broken down. Rinse the cashews and add to blender with the water and flesh from the young coconut, lecithin and agave and blend until smooth. You might need a little extra coconut water, it depends on how mature the coconuts are as to how much liquid will be inside, the younger the nut the more water. Also be prepared that if the coconut is super fresh there will be little to no flesh inside, I always buy one extra to save me a journey back to buy more. Once blended smooth and the coconut oil and cacao liquor and process until mixed.
To assemble your cake you can either, pour the mint layer over the base and allow to set completely. Then pour over the chocolate layer and decorate as desired. Alternately, pour the chocolate layer over the base and then pour in the mint layer immediately and swirl using a chopstick or bamboo skewer. Set and enjoy!!

Zucchini Roll Ups or Lasagne
Two for the price of one, depending on if you fancy serving up a mains dish or canapés then you can adapt the recipe to meet your requirements. If making the roll ups, fill the strips of zucchini with a thin layer of either the sauce or pesto. Roll up and secure with a cocktail stick. If making the lasagne the follow the recipe below.

Serves 2-4 people
Ingredients
2 Zucchini
1 Small Bag Of Spinach
1 Portion of Nut or Seed Cheeze- see page ? for recipe
1 Portion of Pesto- see page ? for recipe
1 Portion of Tomato Sauce- see page ? for recipe

Method
Using a mandolin or potato peeler, slice the zucchini into strips or if not making the roll ups option to slice into small circles. In a dish, cover the bottom with your zucchini, next spread a thick layer of you nut or seed cheese. Layer on top with the spinach or option to use kale chips, followed by another layer of zucchini. Now spread on a layer of the tomato sauce and another layer of zucchini and finally the pesto and one more layer of zucchini. If you have a deep dish you may need to do another round of all or some of the layers. Garnish with kale chips, Spirulina, crumbs from dehydrated crackers or any other favourites.

Raw Cheese Cake

Ingredients
CRUST
1 cup pitted dates
1 cup walnuts pinch of salt

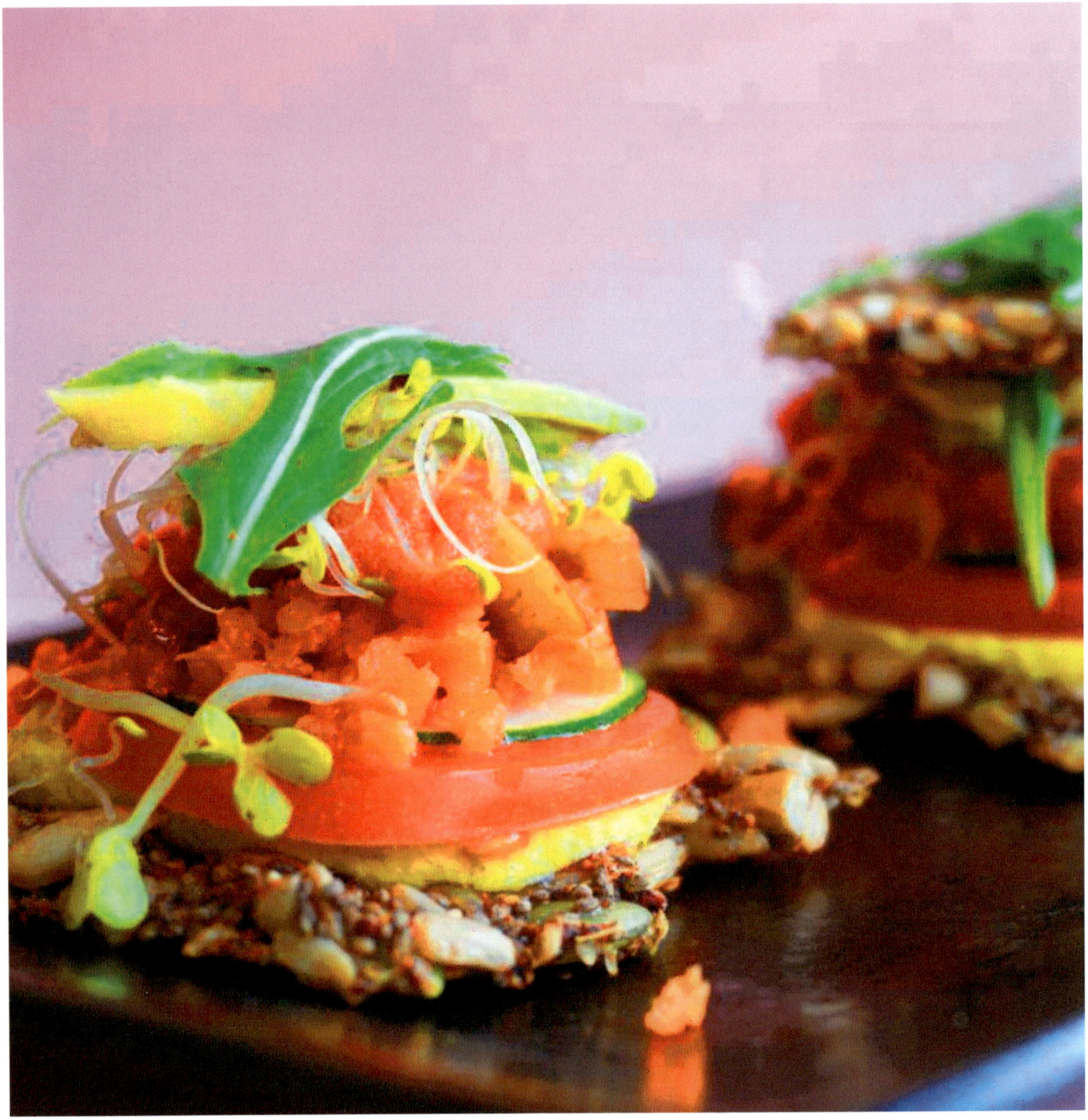

FILLING
1 1/2 cups cashews
1/2 cup agave nectar or maple syrup
1/3 cup melted coconut oil
1/2 cup + 2 Tbsp full-fat coconut milk
1 1/2 cups cashews
1 large lemon, juiced optional extra flavors
 2 Tbsp nut butter either almond butter or peanut butter
1/3 cup of berries, either strawberries, raspberries, blueberries and you can use frozen or fresh

Instructions
Add dates to a food processor and blend and set aside. Next add nuts and blend. Then add dates and blend until it becomes doughy and add a pinch of salt. Grease a 12 slot muffin tray. Next add in 1 Tablespoon amounts and pack it down, I use the back of a spoon to press it down firmly. Put them in a freezer to get hard. Add all the filling ingredients to a blender and mix. Taste and adjust seasonings as needed. If you want to add almond or peanut butter, add it to the blender . If adding berries wait and add on top of plain cheesecakes. Divide filling evenly among the muffin tins. cover with plastic wrap and freeze for about 3 hours leave them out in room temperature to thaw for 10 minutes before serving Enjoy!

Macadamia, Sun Dried Tomato and Rosemary Cheeze

This cheese is absolutely divine, there is something about the culmination of the crunchy texture and creamy, buttery flavour of the macadamias with the intense hit of sun dried tomatoes. Yum! Spread on your favourite dehydrated crackers, inside wraps or on the side of your salad. Macadamia's are a great source of Vitamin A, iron and protein, they are also fab for heart health and contain monounsaturated fats, which may assist in weight loss.
I have fond memories of crunching on macadamias while in Sweden with My friends and Marcus Veda on his retreat. Marcus brought a whole stash of health conscious goodies from his Ocado Order in the UK, I'm actually pretty certain his bag contained nothing else apart from nuts, seeds, superfoods and of course his yoga mat!

Ingredients
150g Macadamia Nuts
25g Sun Dried Tomatoes
1tbsp. Balsamic Vinegar
1-2tbsp. Tamari
1tbsp. Cumin Powder

Method
Add all ingredients to your blender and process. I like to leave a bit of a crunch to the texture, but if you want a smoother result simply process for longer.

I didn't want this to be another 'RAW Food' cookbook that sits on your shelf, but rather an inspiration to follow your heart and your dreams. I have a passion for travel, experiencing new cultures, getting lost in the magic of tropical islands. It's during these adventures that I meet new people, ideas. The food, sounds, cultures open me up in constant new ways. So although you will find many culinary creations in these pages, they have all been part of a bigger story of fun, laughter and happiness.)- Intro

Following a plant-based diet has been revolutionary to me and significantly improved my health, overall well-being and vive for life. I am often asked how I 'got into' raw foods and it's a question which always makes me stop and think. It was as if raw food found me, a journey with no specific searching, just coming into my focus at the right time.

My health had not been great for some time with poor digestion and constant stomach aches. I was challenged by chronic fatigue, a cause of a virus had had contracted form living in a damp and mouldy house in Scotland. Thus meaning every day was particularly difficult to complete a regular routine, that's without even trying to be a mum and work at the same time.

The initial change came from stopping eating meat and fish. I hadn't eaten red meat for over fifteen years, but cutting out chicken and fish instantly improved my digestive health. So much meat contains added hormones and other additives and synthetics, it's no surprise it has such a monumental impact on our health.

My skin had been poor for some time too with outbreaks, which were often painful. The next part of my journey was eliminating dairy and eggs, again seeing a positive shift and my skin becoming much clearer. Onwards and upwards, finally to heal was the fatigue.

I was at a festival and met my now friend, Rachana, who mentioned that she made 'raw' foods. 'What is raw food?' And so my exploration into living foods began. I have learnt a lot through self-research online and books. My raw food guru Kate Magic has inspired me through her courses and online site and her UK retreats. I've been blessed to work alongside Stephanie Jeffs on her retreat in Portugal and I'm constantly expanding my repertoire and being inspired by many other plant based friends all over the world, whom I may meet in person or follow through social media, it does have its benefits.

The more I travel, meet new people and learn new things, the more my concept and outlook of health develops and adapts. I firmly believe that a healthy lifestyle is not just about the fuel we put into our bodies. During my latest trip to Indonesia at the end of 2016, I observed a lot of interesting things, including the fact that the locals love to smoke like chimneys, their staple diet is white rice and most evenings I would say they either drink local beer or a fermented rice wine. Having said this, the majority are in good health and very few are over weight or have access body. They have a good balance of what we may classify as 'unhealthy' with fresh fruit and vegetables, that are picked from either their back yards or maybe a village or two away. Indonesia has an abundance of local herbs, which are known for their healing properties should anyone become poorly. Food is not transported miles and by strangers which disconnects us from our food source as so we know in the UK, where our way of getting ingredients for dinner would be to go to the supermarket.

I'm not suggesting here either that we binge drink or eat more unhealthy foods, simply that we are mindful of our choices and choose what feels good in the moment, not what we think we are 'expected' to do. A lot of the time we are keen to put a label on ourselves, I'm a vegan, I'm a raw foodie, I'm this or that.. More of I am me and I am in tune with what my body needs at this exact moment. The more often we practice listening to our bodies, the more in tune we become with them and the greater our personal health and happiness will become. You will also get to the stage where you can actually ask yourself what would make you happy or not feel too good and have an inner guidance of which route to take at a given time.

The thing I noticed the most is that there is a great deal less stress and a lot more community, family and friend contact. Something I feel in the west we lack significantly, to which there have been many studies carried out, highlighting the negative impact living alone and without support and love from close relatives or friends can have.

The Indonesians work hard, but not to the level where their work overtakes their lives. I know before coming away I was working 6-day weeks, sometimes until late at night and the negative impact this was having on my health. We are lead to believe in western culture that to be successful means being super busy. I know personally many times I have been asked how my business is and my instant reply would be ' Yeah really busy!' Reflecting on this has now made me realise that being worn into the ground from overworking is not a sign of success. A successful business in my mind now, is doing something we love with passion, dedication, attention and detail to the best of our ability. Success is not about working so much we forget to enjoy our lives!

My general conclusion to my observations and self-inquiry over the last few months is that, family and community should be paramount. Yes I know we must work, but there is a way to do this without the pressure of having our 'nose to the grindstone' 24/7.

I always find when I actually take time out, work begins to flow better and the universe provides me with an abundance of amazing prospects for doing what I love doing.

Changes do not happen over night either, but start by making smaller changes. Perhaps spending less time on your phone and an extra hour with family or friends. For me it is to stop working so many 'little jobs' and spreading myself too thin, allowing me to dedicate the time to what I really love doing, running and organising retreats in the UK and abroad. Be kind with yourself, take time to notice the things you do well and congratulate yourself on these achievements. When your focus goes to the positive you will discover more of it flows in.

I followed a raw based diet for 18 months, but after this time felt I had achieved what I needed to in healing my health and that it was actually starting to take a detrimental turn on how I felt. I did not feel as happy, because I was isolating myself from my friends, due to the fact that it wasn't easy to go out and eat or drink the foods I had 'restricted' myself to. I also felt that I was lacking certain nutrients as some raw foods did not agree with me, such as raw kale and other high fibrous foods, which were dense in the vital vitamins and minerals I required. My solution was to lightly steam these vegetables making them easier for me to digest and not getting into a panic if I was out with friends and my salad or meal contained a few cooked ingredients. Wow, what a difference it made to, I started to get my life back, as socialising has always been a positive factor in my well-being.

Therefore I am not here to dictate that you must follow a strict raw vegan lifestyle and diet, it's about finding the right balance for you as an individual. If that means introducing 50% raw with every meal or having a 'raw day', eating 'raw 'til 4pm' and a cooked evening meal, or substituting one meal a day for raw, just listen to your needs and find the groove that compliments your lifestyle and makes you happy inside and out.

So why start incorporating more of these 'raw' style foods into your diet? There are many reasons, not to mention higher energy, greater clarity, positivity, excitement for life and generally raw foodists get ill less and heal quicker if do we do become ill. Plant based foods provide full life force energy, as they are the closest source from sun, transferring this energy into chlorophyll in their leaves which we then use as energy in our bodies, hence why eating a diet high in greens is so beneficial to our well being. When we eat raw foods our body doesn't have to convert anything, it is already a complete energy source, providing our bodies with fuel and nourishment closest to its own source. These foods in their natural state are known as 'Sunfoods', meaning no previous processing has occurred.

ENZYMES- why are these important?

'Plant enzymes are important because they are capable of digesting food before the body's own digestive process begins. In other words, plant enzymes can enhance the digestion of food and the delivery of nutrients to the blood even if you have a compromised digestive system'

When we heat foods above 41c (118f) the content is destroyed and the molecular structure changed, making it a greater complexity for our bodies to break down and digest the food and gain from it the nutrition, which we need for bodily functions, especially digestion.
As children the body makes enzymes naturally, however when we reach adolescence this process stops, and we start to use our collected stores. Meaning we need to obtain our enzymes from another source, that being our food.
A high enzyme diet promotes 'youthfulness'- enough said, who doesn't want that!!

Raw foods have higher nutritional content, when we start heating foods above this 41c it diminishes some of the naturally occurring vitamins, minerals and amino acids, meaning we are not nourishing ourselves as much as we potentially could be. Some other positive factors of consuming a high 'raw' diet are that we generally consume fewer additives and chemicals. Particularly when we source local and organic produce, so not are we only taking better care of ourselves we are looking out for the earth too!! Double win!!

A raw diet is higher in fibre and water- important for hydration, which so many of us are unknowingly deficient in. Our cells are over 90% water so by not being well hydrated we are not living to our full awesome potential. Plant based living encourages a higher alkalinity, you may be familiar with this lifestyle which has received high press over the last couple of years, this is where out bodies again vibrate at their highest and most beautiful frequency.
A diet high in processed foods encourages acidity in the body, causing the cells to become unhappy and creating the perfect environment for disease and illness. These can range from stress, weight gain to decreased immunity. Including a high vegetable content, especially green juices helps to alkalise the body, which in turn creates a stronger

immunity, calmer and clearer mentality. A lot of cooked foods increase strain on the body and immunity, but that doesn't mean you have to go home and sell you cooker, remember everything is about small steps and enjoying the journey so maybe start out with just one day a week raw. It's got to work for you as an individual, emotionally and physically finding that balance, be a 'flexitarian'!! ;) Even by introducing more vegetables and fruit to your diet it's a massive positive- always focus on these and remember we are perfect divine beings doing the best we can in each given moment.

Ok so biggest question… 'What do you eat?', "Do you only eat salads?", and 'Isn't it boring eating only raw?. NO, NO, NO, it's not, there are many wonderful creations to make, have fun in the kitchen with and get exploring!! Focus on the predominant intake of your diet coming from 50% vegetables, mainly greens, lettuce, spinach, rocket, broccoli, kale, celery, cucumber. This is why juicing is so great, as it's an awesome way to easily consume high quantities of these. Green's Contain most minerals and high in protein, so you are prepared to answer that all too familiar question, 'So where do you get your protein from as a vegan'. Where possible eat local, organic and seasonal fruits and vegetables to lessen the impact on the planet, guarantee greater freshness and higher vitamin intake. Be conscious of minimal fruit intake as too many fruits can have a high impact on blood sugars and teeth, which is renowned among raw foodies. I would look at a ratio of 5:2 vegetables to fruit in a day.

The remainder of your diet should be made up of a variety of the following;
Nuts- these are high protein but congesting on system. Always soak to deactivate enzyme inhibitors, making them easier to digest. Eat no more than what you can fit in the palm of your hand per day.
Seeds- these are preferable over nuts, as seeds are easier and kinder to our digestive system and less acidic, try nut or seed butters in sauces or smoothies.
Bean sprouts- nutritious power houses, easy and cost effective do at home- try lentils, alfalfa, seeds, beans- include as much of these in daily diet as possible.
Healthy fats: Avocados, hemp seeds, flax seeds and oils, extra virgin, and coconuts, the last being amazingly nutritious and hydrating, help body to process and prevent storage of other fats in the body and they taste awesome!
Sea Vegetables: Dulse, arami, nori, wakame- easiest to source, kelp noodles, amazing in raw curry as absorb sauce include as much of these in daily diet as possible.
Herbs and spices- experiment try new combos, easy to grow own in windowsill or small pot in garden, get children involved.
Dried Fruits- avoid sulphurs, apricots, figs, raisins, dates, goji berries- these are great added to water to release the nutrients into the water and encourage you to drink more water to nibble berries at the bottom ;)
Grains- buckwheat, wheat grouts, quinoa- can be sprouted, like chickpeas- amazing raw hummus, mung and aduki beans

Sweeteners- so many conflicting stories which are good and which aren't, all have flaws best to keep it varied and use different types, agave, raw honey, xylitol, coconut nectar, lucuma, stevia, apple syrup, date syrup, yacon

Fermented foods- sauerkraut, easy and satisfying to make own, komucha, kefir, kimchi include as much of these in daily diet as possible.

Flavourings- nutritional yeast, miso- not raw but enzymatic activity is living food, tamari/liquid aminos, apple cider, sun dried tomatoes, vanilla, lecithin- brain nutrient only otherwise found in eggs so great for vegans.

Food Combining- avoid mixing protein and starch e.g wheat and oats with seeds and nuts- cause gas and stomach ache also maca and bee pollen.

Avoid mixing fruits with other fruits, avocados don't count and apples are generally ok as easier to digest. Similar fruit with nuts, sprouts and seeds can cause bloating and gas.

Most importantly its about having fun, experiment, try recipes then next time adapt swap ingredients about find what works for you. Useful links: 'Enzyme Nutrition' Edward Howell, www.rawliving.eu, www.happilyraw.co.uk

Techniques

Soaking nuts

Soaking nuts before using them makes them easier to digest. Nuts are more taxing on our digestion than seeds and if you soak both nuts and seeds prior to use for anywhere between 4-7 hours, not only will you be doing your digestion a favour, but you'll also absorb more of the nutrients. To get even more out of your nuts and seeds, once soaking sprout them in a jar or specially designed sprouter for 2-4 days and increase their nutritional content further. Starting the germination process will give your sprouts super powers providing a higher energy and nutritional content. Once sprouted the nuts or seeds can then be dehydrated to activate them and retain this goodness within. Use the seeds or nuts then as required for cake bases, butters or cheezes.

Preparing Irish Moss

Irish moss is great for giving a mousse quality to raw cakes, makes smoothies extra creamy and can even be used in your sauces again to gives that smooth consistency. There are different types of Irish moss and some may require different soaking methods. I buy mine through Tree Harvest suppliers. This type requires around 24 hours soaking in filtered water. Then rinse the moss well before blending in your Vitamix or similar blender. It won't break down completely, so process for around 30-40 seconds with around 150ml filtered water. Use the Moss in your recipe by adding remaining ingredients as directed. Measurements So working with specific quantities in my recipes is not my forte. I'm more of an organic, go with the flow kinda girl!

Making my dishes is all about feeling it, being in the moment and following my intuition. But appreciate not everyone works like that in their culinary creating. Please note that the quantities I have provided are a guideline and I encourage you to have some play time in the kitchen, be prepared to try things a few times and go with what works for you. Most of all have fun!

Printed in Great Britain
by Amazon